What Readers Say:

"I think this book will be a jewel for anyone who wants to get started with planning wealth transfer. More than that, it is a gift for families who haven't figured out the basics of how to get along, appreciate each other for each member's talents or developed the trust needed to be in harmony."

Pete Coors, Chairman
Coors Brewing Company

"Parents concerned about the impact of wealth on their children (and their spouses) need to read this book before they sit down with their estate planners. It's practical, full of wisdom, and destined to become a classic."

Jack Canfield, Co-Author
Chicken Soup for the Teenage Soul
on Tough Stuff ® and The Power of Focus

"This book should prove very helpful to those families embarking on the journey of wealth management. It certainly alerts them to the need for a process of learning and sharing experiences to take place and addresses the need for competent and experienced advisors to help facilitate the process. Our family's experience has led us to an observation and understanding that the process is not a neat serial progression, but more like a plant that blooms, rests for awhile, gathers energy, and blooms more prolifically in its next growth season."

Sarah Ludwick, Owner
Rainbird Mfg. Company

"Preparing Heirs is a valuable book with special thinking about the personal side of family estate planning. It offers good advice as to how to make your personal plans acceptable, helpful, and carried out by the people you love.

I spent my career in financial services, surrounded by knowledgeable advisors to help guide my own plans. I found ideas in this book that had never been addressed before. I thank Roy and Vic for new ideas that have given me some wonderful help in preparing my own family planning."

Glen A. Holden
U.S. Ambassador (R)

"This book will be a very helpful tool for many people who are facing decisions of this type."

Rosemary B. Hewlett

"A powerful statement: '. . . no family, organization can continue to exist that does not share a common mission, common values and authentic trust.' Rather than face a family organization 'death sentence', this book offers a path to successful generational family wealth transitions and healthy family relationships. It provides assistance in turning a parent's worst nightmare into a game plan for generational continuity and tranquility."

Art Ludwick, Owner
Rainbird Mfg. Company

"Few advisors have the gift of turning theoretical advice into an action plan that can improve the odds of success as dramatically as Roy and Vic do in this book."

Jack Wirts, Executive Vice President
The Conference Board

"My first initial reaction in reading Preparing Heirs was that it contained a great deal of common sense. It was more than how to move my wealth...

Money and wealth are not something most families discuss openly. We don't have the tools and skills to do so effectively. "Preparing Heirs" gave us insight with our family and the values we hold but do not necessarily discuss. It's about integrity, communication, and the whole family package.

This book is a Godsend for families who want to stay together long-term and maintain the values and love we all want. The principles of the book are equally applicable on the International scene."

Jose Higueras, Tennis Pro and Coach,
U.S. Tennis Association

"Are your heirs prepared for their philanthropic responsibilities? In this book, the authors help prepare you and your heirs for what may be the most important gift of all. The learned skill of giving."

Don W. Oliphant, Former General Partner
Knott's Berry Farm

"Preparing Heirs is a developed process that continues to be cutting edge in it's design and impact on families. This book is a must read for any family concerned about the impact of wealth on their heirs."

George McCown, Managing Director
McCown De Leeuw & Co.

"This is a valuable and extremely practical guide to do family wealth transfer and management."

James P. Miscoll, Vice Chairman (Retired)
Bank of America

".. 'Preparing Heirs' is a real gem for all those who are striving for successful transmissions of wealth. There is a plethora of books dealing with the mechanical side of estate planning providing expert advice on taxes, wills and trusts, etc., but there is very little in the literature dealing with how to perpetuate the very values which created the family wealth. This book does that in a well organized and easy to follow manner."

Bill Bone
President of a Family Office and a
Family Foundation located in Canada

"When I was a boy, my grand dad said, 'My goal is not to give you the warehouse; it is to teach you to how to keep it full.' Somewhere, while I was earning all of my legal and tax credentials, I forgot. Then, I met Roy, whose constant insistence that I focus on 'empowering those a coming' echoes in my ears during every client conference. Roy's book is a gift of wisdom to those who strive to make wealth an enduring blessing."

Michael D. Allen
Board Certified Estate Planning Specialist

We dedicate this book to the love
most families share, to the peace
and harmony they desire, and to
the leadership necessary to attain them.

Preparing
HEIRS

*Five Steps to a Successful
Transition of Family
Wealth and Values*

Roy Williams & Vic Preisser

Robert D. Reed Publishers
750 La Playa Street, Suite 647
San Francisco, CA 94121
Phone 650/994-6570   Fax 650/994-6579
E-mail: 4bobreed@msn.com
Web site: www.rdrpublishers.com

Library of Congress Control Number: 2002096345

ISBN 1-931741-31-X

Disclaimer

Any similarity to actual people or places is purely coincidental as names and places were altered to protect the confidentiality of our clients and professional associates.

ACKNOWLEDGEMENTS

We recognize it takes a team to put a book together and we acknowledge and thank all those who so generously contributed to "Preparing Heirs."

To the families – We express our thanks to the 3,250 families surveyed, who first shared their family's experiences and results, and the hundreds of families who have been clients over these last 39 years, and their willingness to be open to learn, to grow, and overcome the reluctance and discomfort change can create. They helped us develop our process through trial and error.

To **T.E.C. International,** and especially to **Bill Williams,** the Executive Director and Roy's T.E.C. mates. They were greatly responsible for Roy's early growth in the business world and gave him insight into the very soul of business.

Our grateful thanks to the many friends, clients, and trusted supporters, as well as some of their advisors, who contributed their insight and experience to the book in so many ways. They also became part of the team. Without them, this book would not have its richness.

Dick Boyd, Jack Canfield, Pete Coors, Joe Harper, Jose Higueras, Glen Holden, Art and **Sarah Ludwick, George & Karen McCown, Jim Miscoll, Don Oliphant, Betsy Woolpert,** and **Jack Wirts.**

Specific thanks to those who added so much from their coaching perspective and added to the book's depth and relevance - **Peter Yaholkovsky, Renee Merian, James McManis, Gordon Snyder,** and **Mike Allen.**

Diana Williams and **Rev. Joy Preisser,** who are counselors of the first rank, great sounding boards, and continue to add sensitivity and awareness to our process.

Mike Allen and **Natalie Choate,** both very talented lawyers, who gave us extraordinary analysis as to any inconsistencies in logic and language.

Leslie Yater, for her sensitivity to the issues of wealth and her insight into the process of preparing heirs. **Ruth Schenkel** and **Colin Ingram,** for their editing and doing so on a few days turnaround.

We want to give special acknowledgement to the leadership of **Judith Albino, President, and the Board of Trustees of Alliant International University,** for their constructive suggestions regarding The Leadership Family Institute.

Thanks to all for your contributions!

Roy and Vic

Contents

Tables, Charts, and Questionnaires

Appendices

Introduction

This is not simply another book about estate planning. The reason is simple: we now *know* that transferring "maximum wealth" does not guarantee wealth (or family harmony) in the next generation. In fact, research has established that 70% of wealth transitions fail. [1] Clearly, important elements are missing from the current approach to estate planning, thus allowing this staggering failure rate to continue.

In search of those missing elements, we interviewed 3,250 families that transitioned their wealth. They experienced the same ratio: 70% failed, 30% succeeded. In the course of these interviews, we repeatedly heard three concerns expressed by leaders of these families:

- *"Will our current plan successfully transition family values (and family wealth) to our next generation?"*

- *"How can we prepare our heirs so that wealth is a force for good in their lives, and not a burden?"*

- *"What should our heirs be doing to prepare themselves for wealth and responsibility?"*

In pursuit of answers to these questions, our research separated successful transition families

---

[1] Failure was defined as "involuntary loss of control of the assets."

from unsuccessful ones. Analysis highlighted the missing elements that the unsuccessful families had failed to address with their estate-planning professionals.

All families interviewed were financially successful, and well served by professional advisors who worked diligently to increase and shelter the family assets. Wealth-related issues of preservation, taxation, and governance were handled efficiently and intelligently. But the successful families did a much better job of preparing heirs to receive and manage wealth.

The key missing element in wealth transfer planning was an awareness of *how* to proceed with the preparation of their heirs. The handoff of responsibilities for the family wealth could not be sidestepped, and heirs felt the weight of expectations without the security of preparation. Yet internal family issues around trust, communication, and planning continued to impede the preparation of heirs. This surprising conclusion emerged:

The origins of the 70% failure rate in estate transitions lie within the family itself.

This important finding also implies that answers to the challenge of insuring success in transitioning family values and wealth also lie within the family itself. This confirmed what we have learned and practiced during 39 years of coaching families and preparing heirs. *The Williams Group* specializes in three areas:

Coaching families, family leaders, and heirs
Researching wealth transitions
Educating (The Leadership Family Institute)

Our mission is to help financially successful families overcome the largest unaddressed risk they face: the historical 70% failure rate in estate transitions. Such failures were disappointing to the benefactors who had labored to preserve and build the assets for their children. Failure following the transition proved even more disappointing to the heirs, and severely damaged their self-esteem and quality of life. We now have the knowledge and the capacity to improve the current estate planning process.

This book provides "checklists" for your family to evaluate transition readiness (Chapter 5) and heir self-preparation (Chapter 8), and in selecting a family coach (Chapter 6), etc. We encourage you to jump ahead to the chapter closest to your current concerns.

The pathway to estate-transition success is clearly marked by those families who have gone before. It is their voices and their experiences that speak from these pages. Success ultimately depends on your considered decision to apply their experience for your family's benefit. That's what family leadership is all about. We hope this book is helpful to your family- and especially to your heirs and their families.

Roy Williams   *Vic Preisser*

1 The Future: Wealth Transfers During the Next 50 Years

Who Are The Wealthy?

"The past decade was probably the most exuberant period of wealth creation in human history."[2] *The Economist* reported that the world now has 7.2 million people with "investable assets of at least $1 million." Among the 6 billion people who populate the planet, those 7.2 million people control one third of the world's wealth. Of the 425 billionaires in the world, Forbes Magazine counts 275 of them in America alone. In the face of this growth in wealth, Adam Smith noted 225 years ago that "...riches, in spite of the most violent regulations of law to prevent their dissipation, *very seldom remain in the same family.*" In the face of substantial wealth, accompanied by expert planning to circumvent restrictions on its transfer, transfers of wealth routinely occur. However, the transfers are frequently unsuccessful, "...but not

---

[2] The Economist, June 16, 2001, "The New Wealth of Nations," p.3

always for the reasons that Smith suggested."[3] The restrictions and laws are not the problem.

When Do Transfers Occur?

Wealth transfers are a normal part of the existence of financially successful families. Transfers take place when someone dies, reaches a certain age or state of "readiness," or when other conditions are met. Wealth transfers can take place when health declines or improves, or simply because the current wealth holder believes a beneficiary is "ready." Control is often transferred before the wealth itself is transferred. Control can move to heirs, trustees, spouse(s), or professional managers. An almost limitless range of circumstances can initiate the transfer of wealth or control, but research indicates two major factors drive the majority of transfers:

1. **AGE:** As the years advance for the holder of wealth, and priorities in life are felt to be changing, the holder of wealth moves to assert final decision-making control over HOW the wealth is to be transferred, to WHOM, and WHEN that should occur.

2. **HEALTH:** When a medical event impacts the wealth holder, transfers can occur suddenly. Death, incapacitation, loss of physical stamina, or other health-related events can trigger

---

[3] ibid

wealth or control transfer, regardless of whether or not advance preparations have been made.

For many individuals, transfers occur in an orderly and well-thought-out process. Wealth, or control, is evaluated and positioned for transfer, allocated between individuals, philanthropies, trusts, and the entire process is set into a time frame. Professional estate planners generally focus on taxation, preservation, and governance issues to ensure that the maximum wealth[4] is *available* for transfer. And, if all goes as planned, the wealth is transferred as contemplated. Well executed, a successful plan is a deep and comforting process to the benefactors, professionals in charge of the wealth, beneficiaries, and those responsible for the plan in the first instance. It brings a sense of completion and of preparedness for the next stages in life to the builder(s) of the estate. It helps bring a sense of peace and readiness for life's next stages.

Wealth to be Transferred During the Next 50 Years

The most recent calculations of "personally held wealth" rely heavily on estimates made by the Federal Reserve. The Federal Reserve's estimate in

---

[4] The term "Wealth" refers to assets in any form; liquid assets, the business itself, cash, real estate, stock ownership in non-family-owned companies, etc.

1998[5] cited a figure of $37 trillion. Wealth, as defined by the Federal Reserve, is homes, personal assets, business holdings, real property, stocks, bonds, cash on deposit, etc. Since 1998, changes in valuation, economic growth, and monetary inflation have combined to increase that figure by at least 3% every year. In the year 2003, the amount of "personally held wealth" is probably closer to $44 trillion. This does *not* take into account the astonishing growth (and equally astonishing declines) in the stock market during that same interval.

The amount of personally held wealth expected to be forfeited to taxes, and how the amount available to the beneficiaries (and philanthropies) after taxes, have been the subject of a number of studies and estimates. Perhaps the most comprehensive study of wealth transfer was recently assembled by the Social Welfare Research Institute of Boston College[6] as they developed their prediction as to how much money philanthropies might expect to receive in the future.

That study began by estimating the transfer of wealth anticipated for the 50-year period between 1998 and 2052. The *amount* of wealth to be

---

[5] Issue #5, Sept/Oct 1999 of *The Economy In Action*, Federal Reserve Bank of Dallas

[6] "The New Physics of Philanthropy," Paul G. Shervish, et al, April 11, 2001, Social Welfare Research Institute, Boston College

transferred varied with the assumptions used concerning economic growth rates, taxation levels, etc. The study made "High," "Middle Level," and "Lower" estimates of the amount of money that would be passed on to beneficiaries each year for the next 50 years.

Total Wealth Transfer 1998-2052[7]

High Estimate	$118 Trillion
Middle Estimate	**$56 Trillion**
Lower Estimate	$28 Trillion

This book uses "Middle Level Estimates" throughout. Counting *only* estates with a net value of $1 million or more, the summary numbers for the middle estimate are as follows:

	50-Year Total	Average Each Year
Number of Estates > $1M	13.5 Million	270,000/yr
$ Value of Estates (before Fees & Taxes)	$56 Trillion	$1,120 Billion/yr
$ Value Transferred to Heirs & Philanthropy	**$36 Trillion**	**$720 Billion/yr**

---

[7] Note that the spread between the projected High and Low estimate is about $90 trillion, which is larger than the Middle Estimate number of $56 trillion.

Of the $36 trillion forecast for transfer in the Boston College Study, approximately 33% (about $11 trillion) is expected to go to philanthropic causes either during the donor's lifetime, or as part of the bequest at time of wealth transfer. This is based on assumptions that the rate of philanthropic giving, as well as the proportion given, remains fairly stable.

One interesting statistic from the Boston College study pointed out that the use of philanthropy increases with the size of the estate being transferred. Whether for reasons of taxation or public-spiritedness, the following is forecast:

Estate Size	Percent to Charity
$1 – 5 Million	8%
$5 – 10 Million	14%
$10 – 20 Million	16%
$ 20 Million +	39%

The levels of philanthropic contributions also vary widely from country to country:

COUNTRY	% OF GDP (in 1995) TO PHILANTHROPIC CONTRIBUTIONS[8]
United States of America	1.00%
Britain	0.60%
Argentina	0.40%
France	0.30%
Brazil	0.18%
Japan	0.15%
Germany	0.14%
Mexico	0.05%

The conclusion? A substantial number of family fortunes, either in the form of businesses or other assets, are going to be transferred from one generation to the next- undeniably, the greatest transfer of wealth that the world has ever experienced. Even within the widest range of estimates, the transfer of wealth is forecast to take place at an average rate *of more than $1 Trillion a year for the next 50 years*—and that's only from estates of $1 million or more!

Accompanying that wealth is the unavoidable *annual* transfer of control for 270,000 estates of $1 million or more. This control responsibility falls on designated heirs, trustees, or professional managers- whether prepared or not, and whether

---

[8] John Hopkins Comparative Non-Profit Sector Report for 1995

they share the family's values or not. The responsibility is then redistributed (consciously or unconsciously) across the families (spouses, children, siblings, etc.) of the heirs, as well as among their professional advisors.

The Impact of Wealth Transfers on Heirs

Those who make plans to transition wealth are ultimately concerned about its impact on the lives and well being of their beneficiaries. Our studies indicated that patriarchs and matriarchs shared a similar set of questions and concerns, regardless of whether they were bequeathing liquid assets, businesses, or other combinations. "What difference will the wealth make in the lives of our children and grandchildren?" "Will the family's values underlying the accumulation of wealth be transmitted along with the wealth, and reflected in how the wealth is used?" "How will wealth impact the communities in which they live?"

Clearly these types of questions are not the priority issues addressed by the programs in educational or religious institutions. In fact, there are very few resources that focus on preparing heirs, equipping them to be good stewards and thoughtful administrators. [9] Given the potential for wealth to be used for good or ill, or simply to be "wasted"

---

[9] The Leadership Family Institute of *The Williams Group* performs research on the training of leaders/heirs preparing to assume responsibility for the oversight of family estates.

with no detectable impact, the preparation of heirs to manage wealth becomes one of the major responsibilities financially successful parents face. The question quickly becomes: "How well prepared are those heirs and their families?" Because, in the final measure, the quality of preparation (for the heirs) shapes the outcome to the central concern that seems to occupy the mind of every parent and/or spouse: "Will this wealth help or harm my family?"

Preparing heirs requires a broad spectrum of study and experience. It is not accomplished simply by sending heirs off to college, or even to a specialized business school to learn finance and economics-thereafter returning to manage the family assets. Where does the heir learn how to remain sensitive to (and apply) the family's values within the framework of managing the family assets? The mission for the family's wealth should be a broadly developed consensus mission. Attainment of this mission, accompanied by routine reporting on progress towards the family mission, will build trust and communication within the family and community. That shared family mission brings a sense of harmony to the family and models behaviors for younger heirs, providing them with a sense of family that extends into the subsequent generation.

2 The Uniform Worldwide Failure Rate for Wealth Transfers

What Defines a "Successful" Transfer of Wealth?

The term "successful transition" is defined as "wealth remaining under control of the beneficiaries." If the asset ownership changes form (e.g., the business is sold and the family asset is converted to cash or other form of value), that is a reformatting of wealth, not a measure of success or failure. The same is true for philanthropic decisions where the beneficiary "redistributes" his or her wealth as a voluntary, informed decision. Any combination of taxes, losses, economic downturns, missed market opportunities, litigation expenses, or financial "reversals" occur which *removes the assets, involuntarily, from the control of the beneficiary*, defines the wealth transition as "unsuccessful." Many other definitions could be applied, but this seems to be a definition most wealth-builders use when asked, "What constitutes a successful transition of family wealth?" Following the transition, if the beneficiaries lose control of their wealth through foolish expenditures, bad investments, mismanagement, inattention, incompetence, family feuding, or other causes within their control, then the transition of assets is classified as unsuccessful.

The research continually revealed four major phases to successful transitions:

1. **Development of a family wealth mission, strategy, and roles** (for family members) as guides to those advisory professionals (CPAs, lawyers, etc.) who assist in preparing the transition.

2. **Estate planning and preparation** to ensure that the wealth will transition without being unnecessarily diminished by taxes, ownership questions, unaddressed issues, etc.

3. **Estate transitions** may be experienced in the context of family grief and loss, may not be fully completed for several years, and may involve a number of heirs before reaching their majority.

4. **Post-transition performance** of the heirs/ spouses in carrying out the family wealth mission in the face of inevitably changing circumstances.

With the above steps in mind, let us review the historical success rate for wealth transitions.

What is the "Success Rate" for the Transfer of Wealth?

This question has been the subject of studies over a number of years. Referring to the most recent studies, the Massachusetts Institute of Technology[10] and *The Economist*[11] independently cite the worldwide phenomenon of a *70% failure rate in wealth transitions*. Remarkably, it didn't seem to matter where in the world the transition took place. Countries with no estate taxes, or a "New World Economy" or "Old World Economy," all had similar results – a **70% failure rate from one generation to the next.** This consistent failure rate gave rise over the years to the emergence of "traditional" sayings such as "Rice bowl to rice bowl in three generations" or, "Shirtsleeves to shirtsleeves…" or "Clogs to clogs…" The Chinese have a saying, *"Fu bu guo san dai,"* or, *"Wealth never survives three generations."*

Two major features emerge when the research data is reviewed:

---

[10] Richard Beckhard, W. Gibb Dyer, "Managing Continuity in the Family-Owned Business," *Organizational Dynamics*, summer 1983, AMA, p.5 Author Beckhard was then Adjunct Professor of Management at the Alfred P. Sloane School of Management at MIT

[11] *The Economist*, "The New Wealth of Nations," June 16, 2001, p.3ff

1. The failure rates are consistent regardless of the country, tax laws, or the timing within an economic cycle.

2. The statistic lacks analysis with respect to cause.

Did Any Entity Research the Causes Behind the Failure Rate?

There are no commentaries as to why this failure rate is as high as it is, or as consistent as it is from place to place, and from time to time. While the failure rate of 70% seemed consistent from one geographical location to the next (and thus not different from one economic style or tax system to the next), it was also consistent regardless of variations in the strengths of regional economies.

While causality (of estate transition failure) had not been investigated thoroughly, there were widespread presumptions (about cause) that led to a strengthening of professional competencies relative to estate preparation. Skill building of professionals with respect to the traditional "big three" considerations (Tax Reduction, Preservation, and Governance) have been their best response to the phenomena of potential failure. Written commentaries by professionals routinely highlight taxes that could have been avoided, insurance that could have preserved the transitioning asset, and costly disputes between heirs/beneficiaries regarding who was/is in control of the transitioned assets.

The traditional solutions to the most-frequently addressed issues of taxation, preservation, and governance tend to focus on "competency" issues regarding the selection of qualified estate planners, financial advisors, and administrators. Errors that do occur in failing to prepare for the impact of taxes, the preservation of the transitioning wealth, and the issues of governance and control are usually attributed to the professional advisor (either skilled or unskilled), or to information provided (or not provided) to the advisor by the then-current wealth holder. In other words, traditional concerns have concentrated on *optimizing the advisory process*. This information collection and analysis process began with questions such as "**What** is to be done with the wealth?" (a disposition question), "**When** should the beneficiary come into control of the wealth?" (a timing and control question). Historically, those questions did not presume that there needed to be an inter-generational mutually agreed on purpose (mission) for the family wealth.

The general worldwide environment for estate planning professionals is one of participating in seminars, certification, and qualification for licenses and recognition, and constant improvement of their knowledge and skills. Consequently, professional advisors have become increasingly expert at the tasks of preservation, taxation, and governance of wealth transfers. Clearly, professionals continue to work and improve at their narrowly defined craft-*"Maximize the wealth to be transferred."* On the other hand, given the unchanging worldwide failure rate of 70% in estate transitions, one is led back to Gertrude Stein's definition of insanity:

> *"...continuing to do the same thing,*
> *over and over again,*
> *and expecting different results."*

What Worries Affluent Parents Regarding the Impact of Wealth on Their Children?

Even if the wealth is successfully transferred, and all taxation, preservation, and governance issues have been deftly handled, parents still have major concerns about the impact of wealth on their children. But, the solution to their concern about their heirs (and the spouses of heirs, and the children of heirs) is substantially more difficult to find. The professional "Family Coaching" community is not as experienced, as numerous, and as well established as the financial management and legal professional communities.

The following survey provides an objective summary of the major subjective concerns of affluent parents:

WHAT WORRIES AFFLUENT PARENTS MOST ABOUT THE EFFECT OF WEALTH ON THEIR CHILDREN[12]	PERCENT WHO ARE WORRIED
Too much emphasis on material things	60%
Naive about the value of money	55%
Spend beyond their means	52%
Have their initiative ruined by affluence	50%
Not do as well financially as parent would like	49%
Not do as well financially as parent did	44%
Hard time taking financial responsibility	42%
Resented because of their affluence	36%
Suffer from parent not being around	35%
Date or marry someone who wants affluence	34%
Limited exposure to non-affluent people	33%
Feel they have big shoes to fill and will fail	18%

Many of these concerns revolve around the discomfort that parents feel about the transition of

---

[12] US Trust survey of Affluent Americans XIX, December 2000

family values along with family wealth. The parental concerns address behaviors, knowledge, application of knowledge, and what is often referred to as not-yet-acquired "common sense" and "good judgment." Professionals in those skill areas are often difficult to find. Turning to the Yellow Pages or Professional Directories shows a substantially smaller population of "family coaches" than of "wealth/estate planners." To address these parental concerns it is evident that successful transitioning of an estate requires much more than just the mechanics of taxation, preservation, and governance of that wealth. Decades of court records show professional advisors steadily more competent at taxation/preservation/governance issues, yet the failure rate remains unchanged. To change this failure rate requires looking beyond the existing categories of professional advisors and into root causes underlying failure. The parental concerns listed in the previous table offered a clue because they are grounded in direct experience. Parental concerns continue to circle around issues involving the preparation of their heirs. This point of focus, though historically receiving only minor attention by the advisory community, is replete with a new capacity to dramatically improve the unchanging (and surprisingly low) 30% success ratio.

The next chapter focuses on proprietary research performed by *The Williams Group*. That research has concentrated on determining the *causes* behind the 70% failure rate, and highlighting the differences between families who succeed (in transitioning their wealth) and those who fail.

3 The Underlying Causes of Failure in Estate Transitions

How Can the Causes of Failure Be Analyzed?

The previous chapter emphasized that a 70% failure rate for wealth transitions appears consistent worldwide, regardless of geography or economic cycle. It was also noted the causes for this failure rate were not researched by the collectors of transition failure data. But what about the obvious factors that might be causes of the failure rate?

- The taxation rate levied against estates
- The economics of the region
- Variations in the tax codes of the country involved
- Skill levels of the professional advising team
- Relative size of the estate
- Complexity of the estate
- Unexpected health issues
- Other factors such as:
  - Changes in government
  - Regional catastrophe
  - Cultural practices

None of the above seemed to be linked to the 70% failure rate. The spotlight of the media focused on (often-transient) "newsworthy" issues of the moment, but such shifting focus can give media followers a distorted perspective on underlying issues. The public perceives cause-and-effect relationships when none exist. The media can be misleading as a trend indicator, or cause-and-effect reporter, when individual stories are viewed over the long term.

For example, media attention has frequently drawn attention to farm families auctioning off their equipment in order to pay various (estate?) taxes. The impression is left across the nation that taxes are economically devastating for families. Yet, Professor Neal Harl of Iowa State University declared that in "my 40 years of writing, researching and conducting seminars (for attorneys, CPAs, bankers, and farmers), I have *never* seen a farm business sold to pay federal estate tax."[13] Yet the news continually cites "tax sales" *and* "bankruptcy."

Research into the 70% failure rate led *The Williams Group* to consider three major directions for analysis:

---

[13] Dr. Neil Harl, Professor of Economics, Iowa State University, column of July 25, 2002, internet retrieval, "Federal Estate Tax: Are We Prepared for the Consequences of Repeal?"

Academicians from various institutions have established "Institute(s) for Family Business" to examine family businesses and family transition problems. The academicians sought to define the issues facing successful transition around three major relationship factors:

    Family Members
    Ownership Members
    Management Members

Within these three classifications, academicians studied and defined the group and individual relationships that emerged. For example, the

Management   Family

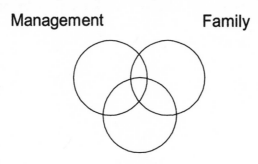

Owners

behavior within a *family group* was predictably different than their behavior with respect to *non-family members*. Yet, even within a family-member group, the relationships changed if some family members were employed in management of the family business and other family members were not.

These intersecting relationships were studied in an effort to give structure to academic analysis, improving the search for predictors of smooth or troubled relationships. While providing a useful referential framework, and helpful in forecasting potential problem areas, the academic model was not designed to deliver answers to the forecasted relationship problems. The method also offered little with respect to which problem or overlapping relationship was most significant. Some insight was gained by classifying inheritance or relationship problems where intersections or overlaps (in the circles of influence) appeared. For example, the difference between a family member who is a part of the management, versus a family member who is not (given that both are owners), predicted that tensions would occur over how much salary the business was paying its managers. This methodology of analysis alerted estate planners to potentially troublesome and divisive issues but offered few tools for correcting the problems. The estate planner's skills were also focused on different areas. Estate planners often lacked the professional training to go beyond (relationship) problem diagnosis and into the counseling necessary to correct the source(s) of the problems. In summary, although institutions improved the identification of the problem, the transition from identifying the problem to correcting the problem has historically been difficult to achieve. Institutions, however, were often effective in connecting family leaders with professional outside resources that could be used to address their relationship problems.

Psychologists came at the problem from a strictly behavioral standpoint, with an understandable tendency to see the family's problems as a series of unresolved psychological (relationship) issues. Some psychologists and psychotherapists focused on parent-child relationships, others on sibling rivalries, and others on the entire family group. Some of the more business-oriented psychological professionals moved into assisting corporations in the design of "Values-Based Estate Planning." This consisted primarily of conversation(s) with the patriarch or matriarch of the family, asking them to articulate their values and intentions, and then attempting to develop wealth-transition documents that reflected those values. Often, this concluded with the design of inheritance mechanisms where the beneficiaries were "protected" against outside or alternative value systems. Heirs were also confined to a structured framework subject to the governance of a trustee. As more than one estate planner told us, "the design of estate transition plans became a task of putting into words what Mom and Dad valued, and wanted their kids to value." As problems were identified, they were related (by the psychologists or psychotherapists) back to earlier relationships, control, and communications issues between parent and child (heir). This led to further counseling, and while it proved helpful to individuals, it left behind the estate planner who was still seeking specific guidance through upcoming troubled waters. The psychological approach proved individually helpful, but failed to provide any generalized answers to the puzzle of why estate transitions failed at a 70% worldwide rate.

Pragmatists *The Williams Group* saw the above dilemma and asked a different question: "What are the measurable *differences* between families who transitioned their wealth successfully, and those who did not?" This simple approach was neither elegant nor psychologically revealing but it did strike at the heart of the problem. *The Williams Group* simply polled many families who had transitioned their wealth. They interviewed 2,500 families, and then examined data on 750 additional families. By the time the study[14] was completed, data was collected on 3,250 transitioned families, and clear differences between successful and unsuccessful families stood out.

---

[14] Appendix I details the research for those who would like to further understand the investigative process.

What's The Difference Between Successful and Unsuccessful Transition Planning?

Successful transitions most frequently included the following:

1. **Total family involvement** (both spouses and bloodline)

2. A **process that integrates** what the family members learn together.

3. The **learning and practicing (in family situations) of skills** in the areas of:

   a. communications
   b. openness
   c. trust
   d. accountability
   e. team consensus building
   f. articulating and sharing values
   g. unifying behind a common mission

The involvement of the entire family proved to be one of the key differences in the successful families. While more difficult and time consuming, it avoided the trap of Mom or Dad dictating "the future" to their children. The research indicated quite clearly that in the event Mom or Dad privately decided (even together) what is to be done with the transitioned wealth, the event of their deaths often revealed open disagreement among the siblings. Each sibling held his/her own opinions about what should be done with the wealth, and felt they hadn't been consulted. This caused a split in generational unity. In these situations, the only unifying factor appeared to be that the siblings often shared the legal expenses of getting the will overturned or the trust agreement broken. (They usually reached quick agreement that family funds can be used to rewrite the edicts of a departed Mom and/or Dad.) In short, it appears unrealistic for parents to expect they can direct the priorities of their heirs, or future generations based on documents developed privately with legal counsel. The most useful mechanism for the upcoming generation to carry on the estate in accordance with parental values seemed to be to involve the family fully in the decision-making process. While the public arena may entrust an office with the responsibility for unilateral decision-making, such as a judge (who can send someone to prison), or a minister (who can accept vows and declare a couple married), the situation is different for family leaders. While great authority is held by a patriarch or matriarch of a family who own/control the family business or wealth in the short term, it is naïve to believe this authority can be reliably projected into the future. Accordingly, parents who make a unilateral decision regarding the heirs and the transitioning of the estate are neither effective or unifying. To keep perspective, when the research suggests that parents "accept the input of the heirs" on the parent's decision, that does *not* mean parents yield authority or control; it does mean giving information to heirs, allowing heirs input and influence on major transition decisions, and for heirs' input to be received with respect and consideration.

A process that integrates the decisions made by the entire family (before death) requires that *all* the elements of the estate plan be addressed. Methods of reflecting the family's wishes and incorporating them into actual binding *documents* are well established. Less obvious is the more-difficult-to-document process or strategy used to achieve the objectives of consensus "Family Wealth Mission." And, following that strategy and structure session, what *roles* need to be fulfilled, who (from the family) is best suited for each role, who wants to take on a particular role, and how do they develop competence for that role?

In short, there needs to be an overarching, proven *process* that will keep everyone on target, translating their individual wishes into a consensus leading to specific estate instructions and actions. When consensus exists within the family, the clarity it provides can dramatically accelerate resolution of the complex decisions that the advisory professionals wrestle with. It also reduces costs of outside assistance because of the focus and clarity that is brought to the process.

Teaching and testing the required skills turned out to be much more important than any of the researchers had forecast. Successful families *knew* what was required (with respect to certain skills) and *also* required that *those skills be practiced, used and demonstrated* within the family environment. In short, the patriarch or matriarch understood that simply "knowing" the right steps was a far cry from "doing" the right steps, e.g., dancing. Almost like an old Arthur Murray dance studio, the steps might be painted on the floor, and everyone might agree that those steps were accurate in describing the waltz—but actually waltzing with one another was an entirely different task. Waltzing knowledge leads to waltzing skill only following actual waltzing practice. Practice is the point in the learning process where knowledge and skill are integrated and applied.

The *process* (and "family coach") selected was important to keeping the decision-making moving ahead, not letting important issues hide, and requiring the participants to practice what they have agreed to preach. With a clearly stated family wealth mission, professional advisors can do their job more quickly and economically. Chapter 4 will have more on this critical topic.

The Garen family had reached agreement on a mission for the family wealth, and wanted the advisors to design a strategy and structure to accomplish the mission. Yet they were concerned about historical professional disagreements between growing the wealth, protecting the family, and minimizing taxes. With the blessing of the family, and with a competent family coach, the meeting began at 9:00 a.m. with the family's instructions that, by day's end, they wanted a wealth-transition plan. The professionals were mandated to reach agreement, that same day, on the outline of a plan that would fulfill the family mission. Failing that assignment, the family announced they had agreed to begin the process of selecting new professional advisors. This was a first for the advisors, requiring legal, accounting, and financial advisors to reach consensus. At the end of the day a plan outline was delivered. All family members and advisors agreed on the plan. The advisors completed the detailed documents in 30 days.

What, Specifically, Caused the Failures in Transitioning Wealth?

Again, not hypothetically, but based on actual research performed on 3,250 families, how did the failed transitions differ in major respects from successful transitions? The breakdown of causes is approximately as follows:

60% of The Transition Failures were Caused by a Breakdown of Communications and Trust within the Family Unit. The term "communication" is broadly understood. Gordon Snyder declares[15] the word "communication" consists of two root words: *"common"* and *"action."* According to his analysis, the objective of communication is to obtain a consensus on "common action" within the family as it influences the transition of the family estate. Common action tends to keep the family aligned with the mission for the family wealth, ensures continuing reinforcement of family unity, and avoids the waste of time and energy (and money) on disputes resulting from separate action, or no action at all.

The Elements of Trust – The term "trust" needs some clarification in this book's research context. A lack of trust does *not* refer to fraud, dishonesty, purposeful deceit, or illegal activity. In the context of this book, the existence of trust refers to whether or not three major components coexist within the family's relationship with its individual members[16]:

1. **Reliability** – do the family members actually do what they say they will do? Do they do it when they promise to do it? Repeated failures

---

[15] Gordon Snyder, LLB, Masters in Taxation, AB Linguistics-Harvard, claims that using this definition more closely resembles the use of communication as a tool for coordinating action among any group of individuals, 1992

[16] Robert Solomon & Dr. Fernando Flores, *Building Trust*, Oxford University Press, 2001, p 134

to live up to promises will establish a pattern of negative expectations, leading to a reputation for unreliability. Promising to be at the recital or at the basketball game for one of the children, then continually failing to show up creates a pattern of unreliability around the person making the (failed) commitments. A label of "unreliable" seemed to be reached much sooner and more permanently than the fact pattern on which that assessment was based.

Leslie had a history of not making meetings with his children, on time or at all. He was a busy executive, running a very large enterprise with six corporate presidents reporting to him. His children loved him but came to know that his priorities were money and business. That did not help their self-esteem. He had a different understanding. He felt he was building his company for his children and they should appreciate and understand this. His continual unreliability in fulfilling his promises (other than money) to participate in their lives sent them a message he did not intend to send. It took three years of rigorous record keeping of his promises and fulfilling these promises to get his children to believe he had become trustworthy (reliable). Of related interest is that, as a consequence of his diligence with his children, his six corporate presidents also noted his increased reliability, as well!

This assessment of unreliability seemed to be unrelated to "reasons why" the parent or family member failed to show up. It really didn't matter to the child that their physician mother was called in for another emergency. The message received by the children was that they were less important than almost anything else and that their parent/sibling/spouse could not be relied upon.

2. **Sincerity** – Does the individual's "internal story" (in his/her mind) match up with his/her "outer story" presented to the world and to his/her family? Is what the world sees of an individual *truly reflective* of the internal individual? Or, does the individual present an exterior that is not in sync with their true interior feelings? Manipulating, positioning, and disseminating gossip within the family usually illustrate this disparity. Insincerity can be evident in false promises, or false offers, or even insincere requests. That insincerity can be accompanied by a lack of commitment to seeing a project through, or being deceitful about the status of progress. The lack of sincerity is often an expression of a lack of confidence within the individual, or an uncertainty as to his/her role and value within the family. This seems to create a "What do they want me to be?" behavior. It is a search for "What will please,"

rather than a search for what will prove personally fulfilling for the individual and unifying for the family. Often, a lack of sincerity can be traced back to a lack of self-confidence. As one leader said, "Insincerity is only a stone's throw away from betrayal."[17]

3. **Competence** – Does the individual have the capacity to accomplish the task at hand? A lack of competence is reflected by a commitment to do something by an individual when the individual simply does not have the *ability* to deliver. In contrast, a deliberately false promise relates to insincerity. Incompetence may be attributable to parents (or heirs) who misjudge their own ability to deliver, and were, in fact, quite sincere when they made the promise. However, a lack of competence is usually caused by a lack of skills, training, and practice in the performance of the task. Of course, different competencies exist for any individual depending on the performing field. I may be a "virtuoso" on the piano and a "beginner" with respect to repairing a home appliance. Competence is, to a large extent, dependent on *not* over-promising, combined with a willingness to invest the time and effort to learn the necessary skills.

---

[17] Robert Solomon & Dr. Fernando Flores, Building Trust, Oxford University Press, 2001, p 134

It was informative to observe levels of competence "at work" as a family leader operated the enterprise and also led his or her family. The family leader had often developed great competence in managing people and processes at work, yet ran into difficulties in applying those same work competencies (and processes) in a family environment. Decisions were made quickly, and the family business leader demonstrated that he or she was a "quick study." But, they also had a tendency to be impatient and have difficulty accepting the (reality of) being a "beginner"...at anything. It had historically been true that the family leader found it easier to hire someone (already skilled) to do something new... rather than to have taken the time out to personally learn the skill. Insofar as it relates to family, one cannot hire someone else to handle issues involving trust. The antecedents of establishing and maintaining trust need to be learned by the family member, and not by a surrogate. This learning cannot be "contracted out" to someone else by the family leader.

Accepting the role and label of a "beginner" is one of the first steps in learning and becoming a role model for the heirs, thus making it easier for the heirs to accept that it is normal to be a beginner. We were *all* beginners at many times in our lives. An heir needs to become aware that life is filled with the need for continual learning. Only when a current family *leader* is open to learn and accept that he or she is a beginner (at something!) will they inspire acceptance of new learning among their heirs. Learning is encouraged when heirs feel comfortable in a role as a beginner, and are not coerced into being a "pretender" at being skilled. Responsibility, forced on an heir, without permission from the family leader to start the new task as a "beginner," is a fearful burden on the heir. The best offset to this fear is for the family leader to model behavior as a "beginner," and affirm that such behavior is normal and unavoidable.

If any of the three components (Reliability, Sincerity, or Competence) are missing, trust is lost. The remaining two are not sufficient to sustain trust in a relationship. All three components must coexist for trust to exist. Many parents are absolutely sincere when they promise to be at the soccer game. They certainly are competent in terms of entering the date and time into their schedules, but their lack of reliability in actually making it to the games, time after time, will erode trust within the family.

Communication within the family also needs a definition to place into context the term "breakdown of communication." Again, going back to the previous definition of "communication," if you are not taking common action as a family, then the activity is closer to noise than it is to harmony. This noise and confusion contributes to the breakdown of coherency in our interactions within the family.

While it is beyond the scope of this handbook, the twin concepts of "perception" and "trust" are also fundamental to communication. Perceptions are based on our experience, history, and the stories we tell ourselves. You may perceive a gesture as insulting in your own country, while I (from another country and culture) may be intending you to perceive the gesture as helpful! If I trust you are trying to help me, I will raise the question when some communication is so obviously out of sync with our conversation and declared intentions. The large discrepancies are not nearly as sinister as subtle discrepancies that pass undetected, and eventually accumulate into a major misunderstanding.

Effective communication means being able to speak openly, honestly, and freely concerning information sought by other family members. Research indicates that family leaders who unilaterally decide that their spouse or children, are "not ready" for certain information are undermining trust within the family. The unilateral decision that an heir is not ready for certain information is clear evidence that the family leadership has not prepared their heir for that information. That may mean the heir, in turn, is handicapped in his or her own efforts at *self*-preparation. How does an heir become "ready" for information on the family's wealth, the parents income, or the appropriate mission for the family's wealth, if the issues and concerns of the parents are not communicated?

Trust is built when the family leaders say, "I want you to know this information as soon as you have accomplished Task X or Task Y." Family members feel entitled to at least understand what is required of them in order to be in the communication loop. Take away that clear understanding and mistrust will develop and undermine the eventual transition of the family wealth.

25% of the Failures were Caused by Inadequately Prepared Heirs. To a large extent, this is a consequence of a breakdown in communication and trust within the family unit. A sudden death within the family leadership, turmoil in the family or in the personal life of the heir, or changes within the sibling group are other factors that cause a precipitous change, catching the heirs unprepared even in families that already had preparations underway.

The preparation of heirs is a long-term task, beginning with the early establishment of family values and developing healthy individual attitudes toward wealth and responsibility. Parental in origin, the establishment of attitudes toward wealth and responsibility appears to be developed during preteen years.[18] Part of this upbringing has to do with the mood the parents bring to the family about money, business, and competition. Do the children interpret money and business as more important than family? One family stated, many times, when the kids were young, they thought that being the President or CEO was "everything." If you were not the President, you were a "second-rater." Competition in sports and school all reinforced this need for them to become "#1." This led to a major problem among the heirs: the team (at school or in the family) was forgotten—only the quarterback was valued.

The skills with which heirs respond to the challenges of wealth are an entirely different set of learnable behaviors that require careful planning during the teen and adult years. Assessment of interests, development of reinforcing experiences, formal education, the ability to track where an heir is in the overall strategy of preparation, the support of the family, and the access to an experienced and loyal mentor are *all* important ingredients in the successful process of preparation.

---

[18] Eileen Gallo, *Silver Spoon Kids*, Contemporary Books, 2001

What was surprising in the research was that many family leaders devoted far more time preparing their estate documents than they did to preparing their heirs for the impact of those documents. While the family leaders may have "learned by doing," the structure and complexity of the assets being handed down had grown substantially, and were no longer amenable to "learned stewardship on the fly."

Family leaders closely examined the credentials of tax advisors, lawyers, estate planners (often hiring two or more firms to compare recommendations), yet gave only cursory examination to the "credentials" of their heirs.

On the day after her 35th birthday, Kristin received a call from a Trustee in another city asking what she wanted the Trustee to do with her "trust income." Unknown to her, her grandfather put stock in a trust for her when she was born and income distribution was to start at 35. When she inquired about the amount of *income*, the Trustee said approximately $500,000 after taxes this year. She and her husband were comfortable, earning $60,000 a year. At age 40, she was to receive half of the principal, and to receive the balance at age 45. Three years later, unprepared for this wealth, she and her husband divorced. The money had emasculated him, and he no longer had the self-esteem to continue in the relationship. They were unprepared, and the best intentions of the grandfather ultimately proved harmful to the family.

The resultant impact of wealth on their unprepared heirs caused the wealth to become a force for disruption in the beneficiary's life and happiness. Obviously, this was not the original intention of the parent/leader.

Only 15% of the Estate-Transition Failures are Attributed to ALL Other Causes such as Tax Considerations, Legal Issues, Mission Planning, etc. In fact, failures of financial professionals to correctly interpret (or anticipate) taxation, governance, and wealth preservation issues were responsible for less than 3% of the wealth transition failures! In short, professional wealth advisors have clearly "come of age" and are proficient at their tasks. The combinations of licensure, professional accreditation, and higher-level organizations (ACTEC, The State Bar, CPA exams, continuing education requirements, etc.) mean that the mechanics of estate transition are generally well understood and offer small likelihood of error for competent professionals. This should give family leaders great comfort in this aspect of the transition of their wealth.

The largest element in this "15% category," although overall much less critical than trust/communication and preparation of heirs, was the **lack of a Mission**. It became clear that those families that had arrived at their professional advisor's office with a *family-developed* mission statement for the family wealth had a clear advantage. Their documents were better coordinated, more up-to-date (in terms of reflecting marriage, divorce, deaths and births), and less costly to prepare and maintain as changes occurred. The sense of mission gave guidance to all the professionals, enabled them to raise solutions at the same time that changes raised problems, and enabled them to coordinate their legal-accounting-investment efforts much more coherently. It also reduced the amount of time wasted by the family having to assemble, gather all the professionals, and sort through the impact of changes. The family wealth mission statement gave the professionals a reference framework for all major issues.

With a family wealth mission, written and built through a consensus process, the professional advisors are benefiting from the following:

1. A family that is in agreement on the long-term mission of the wealth.

2. A reduction in ambiguities of questions on the distribution schemes and how governance, preservation, and tax issues are to be addressed.

3. The roles and actions of the individual family members are set and all have agreed to them.

4. Rapid assessment of how changes in the tax law impact the family transition plan and rapid changes in documents can be made based on mission, not simply avoidance of taxes or avoidance of heirs performing in roles where they may not be currently competent.

5. Family conflict issues that arise can be correlated with the family wealth mission, defining them more accurately, and dealing with them more rapidly and accurately.

Those families that lacked a wealth mission statement, and/or lacked a family consensus behind such a statement, bore the brunt of wealth transition failures. Without a consensus on the long-term mission for the family wealth, the default focus for professionals resorted to that of wealth preservation, taxation minimization, and governance/control. None of these latter three elements are the cause of the 70% failure rate of estate transitions.

SUMMARY: The most important single issue that undermines successful transfers of wealth is the breakdown of trust and communications within the family unit. This leads to a failure in preparing the heirs for their responsibilities. These two elements combine to cause 85% of the failures of wealth transition plans. In fact, less than 3% of the failures are due to professional errors in accounting, legal, or financial advisory planning, or to estate taxes. These professionals are generally very good at what they are trained to accomplish. But most families paying for their advice develop a false sense of preparedness. While tax, legal, and financial planning are essential, they are not the complete answer to achieving success in estate transitions.

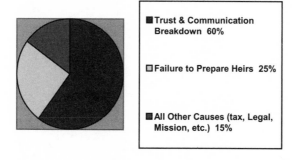

Of every 1,000 estates that were studied through transition, 700 failed. Of the 700 that failed, 420 (60%) failed due to a breakdown of trust and communication within the family. A consequential failure to prepare the heirs for responsibility caused another 175 failures, and only 105 failed for "all other" causes. Within the final category, out of the 105 families that failed for all other causes, only 20 failed because of errors and oversight from all categories of professionals.[19]

---

[19] *The Williams Group*, proprietary research performed between 1975 and 2001

4 Knowing What's Wrong vs. Doing What's Right

One might expect that with all the self-help and "how to succeed" books on the market, this world would be filled with more successful people and more successful estate transitions. With respect to the basic elements required for a successful estate transition, there certainly is no shortage of books on trust and communication. There also is no shortage of information on how to communicate or how to build trust, and there is no shortage of buyers for these publications. Yet the failures attributed to breakdowns of trust and communication continue to dominate the reasons for failed wealth transitions.

Given the often-recited aphorisms, such as "Knowledge is Power" and "Know the Truth and the Truth Shall Set You Free," etc., one questions how knowledge (of the causes of failure) alone can be translated into freedom from failure. In interviewing families, we arrived at the conclusion that most families understood what *should* be done, and what *could* be done, but they lacked the will or the skills to put that knowledge into practice. It was much like *understanding* the precise mechanics of making a basketball shot, while knowing (as a nonprofessional recreational player) that from 25 feet out it is mostly a matter of luck if you get it into the basket.

The U.S. military has understood that gap (between knowledge and proficiency), and so have football coaches and other institutions dependent on teaching effective *team* action. Field-grade military officers attend the Command School at Fort Leavenworth, Kansas as a critical part of their military career development. There they study the past battles and mistakes made by other military commanders throughout history. Then they move to the "sandbox," where they study the battles in three dimensions. Then out to the field for practice maneuvers. Finally, they develop and practice inter-service and inter-country maneuvers *to perfect their skills of execution.* Often they suffer casualties (and even deaths) as they test their ability and hone their skills to perform in the field.

The same is true of a football coach who works from the "X"s and "O"s of the blackboard, to the drills on the field, to the intra-squad practice prior to the actual game. It is only then that the team understands the relationships, the timing, the competencies, and shortcomings of the players, and can thus execute successfully.

The difference between "knowing" and "doing" is large, and it is critical. *That difference can only be bridged by practice*. Practice was most effective when conducted in an environment that was as close to the real world situation as possible. Practice needs to be measured, evaluated, refined, and performed again and again.

The legendary Green Bay Packers of the Coach Lombardi era practiced so strenuously that Sunday's "game day" was privately viewed by the players as a "relief day." They were as prepared as their coach could make them. Winning, as a result of perfectly and intensively executed plays, was natural for that team. Even the Coach of the New York Giants was heard saying to his players, "Practice is what you're paid for. The game itself is just fun."

We concluded that communication among family members cannot simply be comprehended. It must be practiced among the family members. It must be practiced and used as a skill under the most stressful of family situations. This requires understanding, commitment, and discipline from within the family leadership. It is not simply a matter of a patriarch or matriarch declaring, "From now on, we're all going to communicate!" That type of pressure, without training in the skills and without well-coached practice, will simply sow the grounds for deception, false compliance, and mistrust among family members.

How this disciplined practice takes place is a topic of its own, and will be addressed later in the book under the topic of how to go about "Selecting Your Coach/Advisor/Mentor."

5 The First Step, Assessing Your Wealth-Transition Plan

Some owners are transitioning businesses; others are transitioning assets. In either case, the same concern is expressed: "How good is my plan?"

When this question is asked, it sounds different to different people. The lawyer hears one thing, the accountant another, and the children hear yet another. From an individual, professional skill set, their personal viewpoint is not unlike the saying, "For the person with only a hammer, everything looks like a nail."

In fact, the traditional measurement questions for estate planners focus on three major areas of examination:

- PRESERVATION (of assets)

- GOVERNANCE (or control of assets)

- TAXATION (issues that might diminish assets)

These "checkpoints" are so well drilled into estate planners that the percentage of errors and oversights they make appears to get smaller with every passing year. In general, the research showed that professional advisors do a credible job of preservation, governance, and taxation avoidance. As explained in the prior chapter, less than 3% of the failed wealth-transition plans are attributable to faulty planning or poor tax advice, or inadequate document preparation, etc.

What are the Critical "Checkpoints" to Evaluate my Wealth-Transition Plan?

The research suggested two levels of examination. The first level of examination is condensed into a series of 10 (summary) questions that compare your wealth transition plan against the wealth transition plans of those who have gone before you (and succeeded). These 10 questions reflect the conditions that our research has found *directly* linked to successful wealth transition. The weakness of an individual answering the 10-question review is that it is only an individual's perception. The questionnaire does not collect the viewpoints of *all* the family members, and that is an important distinction. Nonetheless, if truthfully answered, it is quite accurate in predicting the family's odds of success (in transitioning their wealth) when compared to benchmarks from similar estates that have successfully transitioned in the past. How many of the following statements can your family answer "Yes" to?

Wealth Transition Checklist
(Written as Positive Affirmations rather than Questions)

1.	Our family has a mission statement that spells out the overall purpose of our wealth.
2.	The entire family participates in most important decisions, such as defining a mission for our wealth.
3.	All family heirs have the option of participating in the management of the family's assets.
4.	Heirs understand their future roles, have "bought into" those roles, and look forward to performing in those roles.
5.	Heirs have actually reviewed the family's estate plans and documents.
6.	Our current wills, trusts, and other documents make most asset distributions based on heir readiness, not heir age.
7.	Our family mission includes creating incentives and opportunities for our heirs.
8.	Our younger children are encouraged to participate in our family's philanthropic grant-making decisions.
9.	Our family considers family unity to be just as important as family financial strength.
10.	We communicate well throughout our family and regularly meet as a family to discuss issues and changes.

Let's examine each of these 10 principles, in detail, and review their relationship to a successful transition of wealth:

Question 1. Does the family have a written Mission Statement that spells out the purpose of its wealth?

This type of wealth mission statement is not the same as a simple mission statement. It focuses on the question of the *purpose* of the *wealth*. For example, is the wealth to provide a level of comfort for the family members? Is it to provide educational and experiential opportunities? Is it to build on for upcoming generations and to fund their business or societal goals? Is it for philanthropic purposes? Or is it a balance between a number of goals? Declaring that the money is to "take care of my wife and children" is what you want to accomplish. *How* it is accomplished, and what the *family* wants to do with the wealth is the purpose of the Family Wealth Mission. It might have specific declarations that set priorities to:

- Create incentives
- Create opportunity for growth
- Empower the heirs
- Encourage community involvement

A mission statement is not just a goal the parents have. It is a *declaration* of the family — a family-wide declaration that can transform the family forever, just as the *Declaration* of Independence changed the relationship of the United States to its countries of origin and the future of the world.

The Family Wealth Mission Statement "DRIVES" the professional advisors, not the other way around.

A clearly written wealth mission statement provides unifying guidance for professional advisors, avoids conflicts, resolves disputes and impasses, and provides forward-looking guidance as new circumstances and situations emerge. It greatly improves the efficiency and cost of the planning process. It enables professional advisors to respond promptly in advising courses of action as new legislation and rules emerge. It goes beyond the preservation, governance, and taxation issues to define the purpose of the wealth, not just its retention. It is not the mission statement for individual family members, or a statement of the family objectives. It is the mission of the family *wealth*. It is not the mission of the family business, or just Dad's mission.

- **A Mission** is the long-term target, the goal, the destination:

  o "Help our family grow as individuals, each fulfilling his/her own destiny"

- o "Offer every child an opportunity to take a role of some kind in managing the family assets"

- o "Share a portion of our gifts through our philanthropy and promote those values our family has developed"

- **An Objective** is one of the steps toward that mission.

  - o "Help family members set objectives for personal learning and growth"

  - o "Identify roles and observable, measurable standards for those roles which heirs may claim, if desired and qualified"

  - o "Help the family develop knowledge and values through their philanthropic activities"

Once a clear mission is in hand, then the strategies to attain that mission become easier to evaluate, measure, define, or change as time passes. While Appendix 2 contains several examples of Family Wealth Mission Statements, the following two examples are illustrative of carefully thought out, heavily debated, and family-wide adopted written mission statements:

"To maximize the equitable transfer of my assets in a way that will enable and encourage my heirs to work for the benefit of humanity."

"Through God's grace, dream, plan, and grow closer to God and each other using the resources entrusted to our care for the benefit of God's work, family, business, people, and community."

Question 2. Does the entire family participate in most important decisions, such as the definition of the Mission for the family wealth?

The key words here are "entire family" and "important decisions." Having the entire family participate, including minor children, begins to set expectations, as well as boundaries. It begins to define, for children, what is expected of them as participants in the discussion. It begins to define the importance of becoming competent on issues on which you (personally) wish to comment. It sets standards for courtesy, consideration, listening, and the inclusion of others. It implies value in receiving a wide range of input and ideas, yet does not lose sight of the fact that the family is gathered to make a decision. Role modeling by the parents, by participative leadership, honest listening, and consideration are all parts of this process. In addition, leadership that is absent from the family meeting is modeling the behavior that says, "My time and personal mission are more important than any of you." Modeling occurs, for better or for worse.

Most importantly, our research shows quite clearly that if the mission (or objectives) are defined *only* by the founders (or leaders) of the family, it appears almost inevitable that profound divergence will occur once the heirs assume (or are assigned) irrevocable responsibility. That not only leads to a difference in mission (among the heirs), but to a difference in strategy, tactics, etc. In short, failure to include the entire family in important decisions, leads to *individual viewpoints that inevitably differ from the "dictated" family mission.* These unchanged viewpoints cause heirs (or their spouses) to use tools of litigation, rejection, nonparticipation, family separation, passive-aggressive behavior, and any other tactic they can bring to bear so their viewpoints are considered-which could/should have been done when the mission was first developed.

The notion of entire family participation is to create an inclusive and considerate environment for all family members and, in turn, to modify and shape some of their more extreme viewpoints. Time seems to temper those individual viewpoints, as does conversational exchange and lifetime learning. People who have lived long lives become more understanding of the human condition, wary of those who have not faced crisis, and patient with the passions of youth. *The earlier this process of participation is begun, the more likely the wealth transition has proven to be successful.*

Question 3. Do all of the family heirs have the option of participating in the management of the family assets?

Of course, the critical word here is "option." Successful wealth transitions always evidenced early inclusion of the thinking and wishes of heirs *and spouses.* The notion that the heir will be responsible for assets once his or her parents are gone from the scene is a consistent estate-planning pattern. The objectives are to reach out to the heirs, early on, and begin to prepare them to:

1. Be concerned about the quality of management of the family assets and,

2. Know that heirs *can* have a role in the management of those assets based on their level of competence and interest.

The size of the role an heir plays is determined by his or her competence, reliability, sincerity, and interest. Certainly one would not urge that a family member who was competent solely as a portrait painter should be saddled with the daily management of overnight, interest-bearing investment accounts, or the performance of hedge fund managers, etc.

In the first meeting of the Davi family and their "coach," all family members attended. One 30-year old heir was two hours late and did not appear to have bathed for some time. He had not had a steady job since college and the family openly referred to him as "the loser." During 18 months of periodic family meetings to build trust and communications and a family wealth mission statement, the family discovered that, because he had no interest in the family business, they made him feel that, "If you were not a businessman, or President, you were nobody." However, when the discussion and planning got to philanthropy, the heir saw possibilities for him to work in a different environment. He blossomed. His energy and enthusiasm for the potential within the family foundation was contagious. He plunged into the role, working feverishly to learn more and become competent to make "good" philanthropic decisions. Eighteen months later, after a series of family meetings, the now well-groomed heir was named the President of the Family Foundation and was running 5K marathons. The transformation was truly spectacular.

But rather than cause the heir to feel separated, unaccountable, or unimportant in relationship to family assets (on which the heir may depend), one needs to assure each heir that there *is* a role they can play. It is a matter of defining that role, and preparing the heir for that role. The portrait painter might play a role in overseeing a family philanthropy devoted to supporting the arts. In that role he/she could evaluate the impact of the family's philanthropy dollar, better uses for the philanthropy dollar, and discuss new opportunities. Options to participate must be created for heirs. Deliberately include heirs instead of rigidly and automatically excluding those who do not *appear* to fit in.

Question 4. Do all heirs understand their future roles, "buy into" those roles, and look forward to performing in those roles?

On agreement with respect to the family wealth mission, a strategy and structure for attaining that mission is developed. Once the strategy and structure are defined, then roles (for heirs, spouses, etc.) with observable, measurable standards need to be defined to carry out that strategy. With the roles defined, successful estates then called for "expressions of interest" in personal conversations with each of the heirs. Some heirs wanted to be involved in the family business, others in the family philanthropy, yet others sought roles as the managers of real property or cash assets, or the management of the family's money managers.

Critical to the process of these successful families was the matching up of the heirs' *interests and competencies* with the roles that were available.

Of equal importance is that no heirs of successfully transitioned estates were ever "pressed" into their duties. No one was forced into a responsibility. There were sudden deaths or departures that occurred in family management structures, and successful families would often bring in temporary managers (family and non-family). Those temporary managers came with the clear understanding that this was a special situation, that their tenure was expected to be temporary, and that an active search would be underway to determine the best replacement. Yet that temporary manager often transitioned into a full-time mentor to the heirs who eventually replaced them.

The careful assessment of an heir's *interests*, and the proper match-up with the family's *needs*, is important to the heir's long-term satisfaction and performance in the job. In addition, where heirs "bought in" to their roles, the necessary preparations, and the heir's active participation in developing their own competencies seemed to follow.

The successful families agreed that early awareness and preparation of heirs for clearly defined future roles brought a great deal of *stability* into the family. This was in contrast to the turmoil of heirs "jockeying around" for roles as their interests changed, new spouses entered, roles changed, and the strategies adjusted.

Heirs' interests will change. Heirs mature and refine and redefine their individual objectives at several points in their life. Accordingly, the successful families seemed to keep the communication channels open by meeting with the heir from time to time. Those meetings privately checked the heir's "temperature" to see if the heir remained interested and was making expected progress in developing the necessary competencies. If the family leader detected a waning of interest, or a failure to keep up with the requisite competency development, then it was time to reassess the role and direction for the heir, and to discuss that openly and directly with the heir. Such a discussion proved to be a relief, not a burden, for the heir. The heir was usually the first person to realize that he/she was falling behind the progress curve to which the heir had agreed.

Question 5. Have the heirs actually reviewed the family estate plans and documents?

Whether or not an heir has a law degree, this question goes to the issues of communication, openness, and instilling a sense of responsibility in the heirs. Actually reading the words and seeing the numbers has had a surprising impact on heirs and benefactors. As Samuel Johnson once wrote: *"Depend on it, sir, when a man knows he is to be hanged in a fortnight, it concentrates his mind wonderfully."*[20] Not that a hanging is in store, but the reality of planned responsibility (as a steward for some portion of the family wealth) hits home when it is actually seen in black and white.

All the Stanley family members participated in developing and setting "Inheritance Standards," including grandchildren age 14 and older. The heirs-to-be were, frankly, startled to be allowed to read the resultant wills and documents which stated: "The children must be employed 5 years prior to receiving any financial distribution, they must have received increased work responsibility and be paid accordingly. If they fail to achieve these standards, they have one more 5-year time period to meet the employment-promotion requirement, and if they cannot, the funds will revert to charity." The parents were delighted by the family-wide support for the development and acceptance of the proposed standards.

We have also seen heirs who, on viewing the will and relevant preconditions, revealed to their parents they had medical reasons why they could

---

[20] Samuel Johnson, "Boswell: Life"

never bear or sire a child. This avoided a futile (but historical family standard) "childbearing condition" in their inheritance entitlement. Again, it goes back to the policies of inclusion and openness for the family.

Children who do not know the extent of the family's wealth can never discuss what they might be inclined to do with it when it is inherited. Adults who read conditions that they feel are onerous or intrusive can only discuss those feelings with their parents while *all* are still alive. Often these discussions open dialogues that prove to be among the treasured moments parents later recall.

One additional finding from the research: Parental fears of wealth creating a "disincentive" disappear in most cases as the growth and personal development of the heirs take place and the heirs experiences the parental assessment of recognition, appreciation, and acknowledgement of achievement.

Finally, as the communication and trust increases, even sensitive issues can be discussed openly with the help of a coach. This takes a great deal of finesse and skill so no one is offended or embarrassed. Issues of being gay, unfair distribution of assets, perceived grievances, or even the inability to conceive a child can create difficulties in communication.

In the coaching process, family meetings on developing the mission, structure, strategy, and role selection uncovered most (previously hidden) concerns held by both the heirs and the parents. The important conclusion here is that parents who involve the heirs in the documents, providing them to the heirs for review and comment, are uniformly more successful in family wealth transitions than those parents who reserve the documents for themselves.

Question 6. Are current wills, trusts, and other documents directed to make most asset distributions based on heir readiness, not heir age?

Tradition and certainty die hard. Because it is easy to measure age numerically and with specific dates, precise asset distributions are often based on age. This, in spite of the fact that research indicates that parents understand their heirs vary widely in terms of maturity, preparedness, readiness to make use of the assets, etc. Simple rules such as "1/3 on the 21st birthday, 1/3 on the 31st birthday, and the final third on the 41st birthday," are easy to reflect in documents. In the event of unforeseen changes required for health reasons, marriage/divorce reasons, sibling-aid reasons, or any of a number of circumstances, estate planners often build in the ability to vary some conditions. One cannot construct a document that would be able to respond to *all* possible eventualities, and flexibility tends to broaden the language, which increases the trustee's legal liability in the event of a "wrong" decision. This is why most distributions fall back on precise ages and dates for entitlements. In contrast, the most successful estates transitioned wealth based on a series of events or *accomplishments*.

As stated earlier, one family developed a standard for being a beneficiary of the estate: At age 35, the first distribution was allowed, but in order to qualify for the distribution the beneficiary must have been *"fully employed for the 5 preceding years, must have received increases in responsibility with pay commensurate to that responsibility."* These were observable and measurable standards. If the beneficiary had failed to meet the preceding standards, they received an "extension" for another 5-year period. If they did not meet the standards during the extension period, then they were not allowed to become a beneficiary and their funds were given to charity.

The most successful standards observed were those developed by the entire family as part of the overall strategy/structure development. Standards built around what parents admire about their children are much better than the simplistic chronological standards of age. One family said: "We saw the precision of age as the lawyer's refuge."

Some families and professional advisors are opposed to "standards," but when the *entire* family develops them and *agrees* to live by them, they work well. Age, alone, should not be the qualifier.

As Ponch Sorenson entered his late 80s, he began to rethink his years of hesitation about turning the business over to his only daughter, Karen. She knew the business, having worked there all her adult life. He was slowing down, tired more easily, and couldn't put in the 12-hour days of only a few years ago. He had held tightly to the reins of leadership, and kept her from becoming the company President of the family corporation, but now, with Ponch's advancing age, he knew she'd *have to* take over.

Ponch called Karen into the office and made the announcement that he was finally promoting her to President. She was "ready" and so was he. He was shocked when his daughter said: "Daddy, I'm 65 next week and scheduled for retirement. Maybe one of the grandkids might be interested, but one's a doctor, and the other's a musician. I doubt if they're interested in giving up their professional careers."

The "accomplishment method" proved to be a motivator and was related to qualifications. The "date method" was simpler and legally less challengeable. The successful wealth transitions emphasized the motivating "levels of attainment" methodology, while the less successful transitions relied solely on age and dates.

Question 7. Does the family mission include creating incentives and opportunities for heirs?

Successful family wealth transitions included these factors to build a sense of "fun" and "involvement" for the heirs. Rather than entering a dependency relationship, or a form of family welfare by giving each heir $20,000 each year, the family leaders went out of their way to develop ways for the heirs to *earn* that same amount each year.

Frequently, the family leaders gave each of the heirs steadily increasing responsibility for a specific amount of the family's wealth- $50,000 to $1 million. The family interviewed money managers (with the help of a coach) to work with the heir. The chosen money manager and the heir managed these funds based on the Investment Policy Statement the family and heirs developed with the coach. The money was invested, the heir monitored the process monthly, and reported quarterly on the results. At the end of the year, it was agreed that the family leaders and the managing heirs would *split the profits. It surprised everyone how often the profit split was about equal to the annual gift exclusion allowed under the IRS code.* Instead of doling out welfare, and a decrease in self-esteem, both the heir and parents built competence and confidence.

In another case, a young heir was given responsibility for a number of decisions regarding the family foundation. *If* she set standards for performance (to accompany each grant given by the family foundation), *and* selected charities that attained those standards, *then* she was given more funds to allocate the next year.

These simple incentives linked performance to reward, kept communication channels active and open, and built self-esteem in the heirs. Incentives also taught that heirs will never know everything they would like to know, or need to know. They build a sense of continued learning and an appreciation that the rewards go to those who "mind the store."

Question 8. Are the younger children encouraged to participate in the family's philanthropic decisions?

The successful wealth transition families using this practice did so because it was the forum for discussing family values. Children, beginning around age 10 to 12, were encouraged to talk about what they felt was important. In translating their concerns (values) via the family foundation, the parents taught them the importance of family values, and the importance of accountability (following their family's contributions to see if the money did what it was supposed to do). The heirs gradually learned to ask questions, came to expect accountability, valued feedback and reporting. They began to shift their charitable interests by concentrating their contributions to the most responsive and effective charities. Items such as the charity's ratio of direct to indirect expenses and what portion of its funds went to fund-raising, and what portion went to the purpose of the charity became important issues. These issues in turn fostered increased family discussion, and a steadily increasing sense of the family's values as young heirs came to know more about the family's charitable acts. Over time, family members came to depend on the younger heirs for these major philanthropic decisions and it proved to be a fertile training ground. This also was extraordinary training for the children with respect to family values and substantially accelerated their skills at translating family values into individual action and decision making.

Question 9. Does the family consider family unity to be just as important as family financial strength?

This issue was known as the "balance point" for successful families. Focusing *solely* on passing the *maximum* amount of wealth to the children deprived families of the time needed to build relationships and to reach agreement on the mission for the family wealth. Failure to involve the entire family in mission planning, and future decisions on strategy and roles, diminished the sense of family unity. For those money-focused families, they previously had decided that any money spent for professional teaching and coaching of heirs was "an avoidable expense." They declined to invest the resources to prepare their heirs. Once the wealth transition occurred, the *costs of disagreement*, and the resentments concerning competence, quickly surfaced among siblings, spouses, and cousins. The families successful at transitioning wealth devoted a great deal of time to maintaining a unity and harmony within the family. Family squabbles did occur, but the successful families focused first on family unity, and second on maximizing the value of the assets to be transferred. Successful families uniformly focused first on building relationships, based on authentic trust and open communication. They knew that if they could accomplish this, the accumulation and wise use of the family assets would be handled well. They saw the mission, common values, and trust as the essential foundation for growth and family harmony. Tying this to the broader mission of their philanthropic goals brought balance and even served to reinforce spirituality[21] within the family through the generations. The ability to articulate these priorities to the family members, in family meetings (and with individuals), left no sense of ambiguity as to what Mom and Dad wanted for the heirs. It taught the heirs to get over the dispute, work for a mutual resolution, and get on with their lives together. Parents who simply "gave the order" to "get along" were singularly unsuccessful. They required professional assistance from outside the family to make this happen within the family. Families, themselves, almost always lacked the skills to make this happen in isolation. Successful (transitioning) families inevitably brought in *outside professional "coaching" help*, just as they historically did with lawyers, accountants, and estate planners (and driver training for their teenagers). "Family comes first" seemed to be the motto of families that were successful in transitioning their wealth.

---

[21] In this book, spirituality means values such as unconditional love, seeking first to understand then to be understood, and the feeling that there is a higher calling to life, demonstrating a long-term purpose for existence.

Question 10. Does the family communicate well and regularly meet as a family to discuss issues and changes?

The leadership of families that had successful transitions seemed to share certain rules of communications within the family:

1. No business meeting was so important that it could not be interrupted for a phone call from a family member (who, in turn, was encouraged to call outside business hours);

2. The family routinely met for seasonal get-togethers on Christmas, Hanukah or other holidays, plus a once-a-year scheduled family meeting to discuss business issues (separate from holiday get-togethers);

3. Communication involved the entire family, including spouses. It was open and everyone was sought out for thoughts, opinions, and recommendations. The topics most frequently discussed in successful family meetings dealt with forward planning and informing the family of newly shared responsibilities and business/asset developments. The family meetings were usually one- or two-day affairs, with absolute confidentiality maintained within the family, and strong efforts made by the

leadership to make certain that everyone was heard.

Families that failed transitions also had family meetings, but their meetings were usually unsuccessful. Unsuccessful meetings tended to be called and led by the family leaders who were unskilled in "coaching" or "facilitation." These family leaders developed agendas (usually their own issues and priorities) and dominated and controlled the meeting. In those situations, the heirs felt it was "lecture time" not "participation time." Some felt they were being programmed or controlled and felt these meetings were a waste of time and money.

Unsuccessful wealth transition families combined family meetings with holiday events, and tried to control the meetings with a firm grip, often leading to high levels of stress and anxiety throughout the (holiday) meeting. It seemed to be a bad idea for the patriarch or matriarch to personally lead the meeting or to try to mix "professionally coached" family *meetings* with family holiday *gatherings*. Family meetings could be held effectively during gathering period (holidays, birthdays) but only when held separate from the celebratory gathering itself.

How are the Answers Scored and Compared to other Wealth Transition Families?

Historical data from the 3,250 families enabled us to confirm the importance of the 10 checklist items by comparing the answers of successful transition families with those who were unsuccessful. In general, they divide into three areas of comparability:

- **Families able to answer "yes" to 7 or more of the 10 questions** above are closely correlated with those families who have successfully transitioned their wealth. They are most likely the one family in three who will transition their values and their wealth into a relatively harmonious environment for the benefit of their children and grandchildren, while preserving a family unified in its belief that the individuals in the family are just as important as the wealth in the family.

- **Families that are able to answer "yes" to 4 to 6 of the 10 questions** are likely to benefit substantially from efforts to improve the levels of trust and communication within their family. This is fundamental to preparing their heirs for wealth and responsibility. In the absence of a substantial effort, however, this group will remain most closely correlated with the 70% of the families who do *not* effectively transition their wealth. This is the "high return" group that can achieve the largest improvement in their transition odds of success with the least amount of work.

- **Families that are able to answer "yes" to only 3 (or fewer) of the 10 questions** above are closely correlated to those families who failed to successfully transition their wealth and values. Those families are characterized by a dissipation of wealth among the heirs, infighting and hostility within the family, and a loss of family unity in the following generations. It should be clearly understood that those situations *can* be changed for the better. It is simply a matter of family leadership and professional coaching assistance to make the changes necessary to increase the odds of a successful transition. For this group, a substantial amount of work is required.

"Problems cannot be solved by the same level of thinking that created them."
—Albert Einstein

Getting Input From The Entire Family, Without Fear and Guilt

If the score attained, by an individual, on the 10-Question Transition Checklist raises concerns, the next step is to look into the *entire* family, in more detail. The 10 wealth transition questions are strong indicators, with high reliability in their correlation with successful families and unsuccessful families. The 10-question reliability level is further improved, *and the problem areas pinpointed*, if the *entire* family (including spouses and adult children) is given the opportunity to separately answer *a more detailed set of questions*, and their responses are used in analysis and correlation.

With 50 expanded questions answered (anonymously) by all family members and their spouses and adult children, the analysis has approximately 10 times the information to work with. That analysis will identify:

- Specific areas of disagreement within the family

- Specific variances within the family with respect to the family's sense of :

  o Trust and communication

  o Heir readiness for responsibility

o Shared understanding of the family wealth mission

Another reason to seek responses from the entire family is that often in families where there is a shared ownership in the second generation between brothers and sisters who inherited ownership from a founding parent, there can be even wider disparities within their (third generation) heirs in each of their families.

Most frequently, tensions exist between the heirs from the *operating side* of the family (e.g., the daughter of the founder who is running the family business), and the children of the *non-operating side* (e.g., the other daughter of the founder who is *not* running the business and is a passive recipient of income). This is also true for those in the family who are managing assets versus those who are not involved in the management of assets yet are "passive" recipients of income from those assets.

The family 50-Question Survey, combined with individual interviews, can reveal where areas of mistrust reside, where the communications are lacking, and who in the family feels included or excluded. These are critical pieces of knowledge, which must be dealt with if the upcoming generation of heirs is to experience a successful transition of the family wealth. Without addressing these problems, "shirtsleeves to shirtsleeves" in three generations has a high probability.

The copyrighted 50 questions, as well as the methods to analyze the responses, were developed by *The Williams Group*. It provides an accelerated response time for families seeking rapid answers/action on wealth transition concerns. While the detailed questions are not included in this book, an example will illustrate the expanded questionnaire's potential.

An example of the analysis from the 50-question all-family survey: The individual responses to this questionnaire are kept anonymous, even among family members, to avoid challenges to any individual's answers and to ensure the highest degree of candid response possible. Below is an example of a "Pre-Coaching" bar graph developed for a family who called their family group "MOUNTAIN." The family members who responded are labeled A through F across the bottom of the graph. The graph represents responses of the parents, children, and spouses. The three major aspects measured by the questionnaire are:

- Trust and communication levels ("T&C")

- Heir preparedness ("Heirs")

- Mission clarity for family wealth ("Mission")

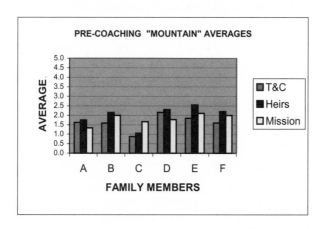

"Perfect" would be a score of 5 and a minimum of 3.5 for all family members in every category. From the graph above, it is evident that the Mountain family was operating with a generally low level of **trust and communication**, since the highest score (D) was a little over 2, and the lowest (C) was less than 1. **Heir preparedness** was perceived by the family as high as 2.5, and as low as 1. Finally, the **mission of the family wealth** ranged uniformly low, between 1.5 and 2. In short, *everyone* in the family felt unprepared for the transition (even the parents) and the spouses/heirs rated their needs for assistance as relatively urgent. This led to a prediction that, on transition, there was likely to be litigation and a breakdown in the family unity. Their lack of trust was literally preventing everyone from declaring their "beginner" status, thus preventing learning, preparation, and improvement in the family's odds of a successful transition.

These findings, combined with subsequent individual interviews, clearly pointed out the need for and the direction of remedial actions for the family. The patriarch and matriarch called a family meeting, scheduled a series of meetings over the upcoming year, and brought in skilled family coaches. The family, as a unit, went to work on clearly identifying problems and focusing on clarifying the mission for the family's wealth. The patriarch and matriarch were surprised to discover how many values were shared among their heirs, even in the context of mistrust that hovered over the gathered family. The family then turned to the coaching team and began work on building bridges of trust and communication within the family, dramatically improving their ability to talk with and help one another. Finally, they turned to the task of preparing the heirs. Moving on to the analysis of heir interests, then to the evaluation of competencies, and finally to the development of individualized programs and individual mentors for each heir. After a concerted family effort in a series of six (two day) meetings over a 20-month span, the post-coaching results showed a remarkably improved picture. While the complete "post-coaching report" is shown in Appendix 2, the post-coaching graph shows obvious improvements in each of the three categories. Trust and communication improved remarkably as a result of well-run and professionally led family meetings. The overall assessment of the readiness of the heirs was much improved, leading to greater trust in the competencies of the heirs-and a much lower likelihood of costly post-transition litigation. Finally, the clarity of the mission was obvious to all, and will serve as a guidepost for future communication and heir performance assessments.

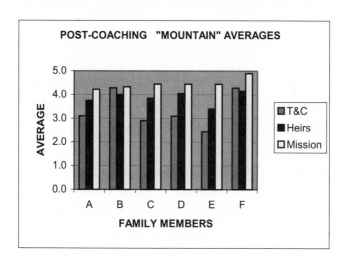

The family functioned better and was certainly more harmonious. Disputes and family friction eased, and the stable transition of wealth seemed much more probable. The family continues to work on the basics.

SUMMARY: There are now powerful analytical tools privately available that can identify the sources of family conflict. A simple 10-question poll can accurately indicate a family's odds of success in transitioning wealth.[22] A more detailed 50-question poll, taken anonymously by *all* family members and their spouses, can identify (with better than 90% accuracy) *specific areas* that will benefit from attention. Skilled family coaches (who are not necessarily lawyers, accountants, psychologists, estate planners, or trust officers) can make use of these analytical tools to identify areas where harmony is threatened within the family. Increased harmony is founded on increased trust, improved communication, a shared mission for the family wealth, and carefully prepared heirs. The odds for a successful transition of wealth are dramatically improved *only* if the patriarch and matriarch take action. Simply knowing what is wrong is not a solution. Simply knowing what needs to be corrected, or even how to correct it, is not a solution. Skilled coaching assistance is required for a family to personally experience a

---

[22] Appendix 4 provides information on obtaining questionnaires for your entire family.

different way of interacting that will ensure a greater probability of the successful transition of family wealth.

6 The Second Step, Taking Action on Transition Plan Deficiencies

Knowing that Changes Have to be Made

Fishermen don't rely on the same fly for every fish. Hunters don't always wait in the same location. Business people don't run the same advertisements time after time, even if past advertisements have been successful. Change is *necessary* to remain competitive, and to sustain vitality in an ever-changing environment.

There is intrinsic satisfaction and enjoyment in learning, having new experiences, and engaging the powers of forecasting and anticipation. Yet people resist change. Change is work. Change is required in life.

For most families that have done a preliminary assessment of their estate transition situation, the answers they received may have been unsettling. The answers may predict that unless they initiate (and follow through on) change, the odds of a successful estate transition are in the 30% range;

and unless a cooperative learning environment is created for the next generation, it's only a 9% success rate by the third generation (30% x 30% = 9%). If the family can make some changes, they will move the odds up into the 70-90% range! How is this accomplished?

Once the family leader has self-assessed his or her odds of a successful estate transition (the 10 questions of Chapter 5), they generally find themselves:

- **Grateful** for knowing where they stand

- **Concerned** about the low odds of success

- **Curious** about how to begin needed changes

Steven Covey writes that "...people will **not** do what's in their own best interests if it makes them uncomfortable." That is a major reason why change is difficult to achieve. We become comfortable in known environments and repetitive situations that we have gathered as a way to leverage our personal strengths. In fact, we unconsciously "fortify" our environment and processes against outside disruption, all in the name of "focus." And at some point later in life, leaders/parents often begin (quietly and privately) planning a peaceful and "fair" distribution of the fruits of their lifetime of effort. It is uncomfortable for parents to talk with children about parental thinking, their personal plans, their concerns for each of the children. So parents do their planning in private with the help of their trusted lawyer, accountant, and estate planner/investment advisor.

How many changes are as challenging in their children's lives as the sudden responsibility of wealth transferred from a recently departed parent? The magnitude of the change, in itself, creates a powerful impact. Parents frequently compound this dramatic change by deciding the wealth transition in isolation from the children. Under these circumstances, the distribution of family wealth is potentially harmful to the heirs. The heirs have not been prepared for wealth and the responsibility that accompanies it. The irony is that the fruits of the parent's labor usually turn out to be a powerful enough force for change that, if the heirs are not fully prepared, the fruits can prove toxic to the heirs.

The process of widespread family (and spousal) involvement changes that equation. Our research clearly indicates this is so. Family involvement helps all family members see the importance of the development of competency, confidence, and self-esteem in the heirs. They see the open communication and authentic trust established within the family unit and see heirs begin to take roles that will fulfill the family mission. This lets the family leaders know that their lifetime of work is in good hands.

When businesses reach conclusions about their *products*, they act in deliberate haste. The faulty *product* is superseded; the *material* that becomes illegal or ineffective is recalled or replaced; the *contract* that is lost is replaced with a new sales effort and outlet; the imported *raw materials* that have been cut off require a change in process, pricing, or supplier. Everyone bends to the task of correcting the situation as soon as possible. The U.S. Navy refers to this total response as "General Quarters." When the ship's alarm sounds "General Quarters," every able-bodied member of the crew responds to emergency stations ready for priority responsibilities and additional duties as necessary. The resources are rallied, and action is taken. The life of the ship is critical to the life of its crew, cargo, and mission.

Dealing with family issues that threaten the orderly transition of family wealth and responsibility is no less critical. It is a matter of rallying the family and outside resources to address the largest risk of all: *That the hard-won family estate may not transition successfully.*

In fact, given that 70% of estate transitions fail (and *not* for tax or legal or insurance reasons), *managing the failure risk* means focusing on the issues of trust and communication, preparation of heirs, and defining mission/structure/role. Experience of 39 years has repeatedly demonstrated to the authors that the rallying of family resources for the purposes of developing and acting on a clear plan of transition is one of the most welcome events we see a family experience. It is a signal that the family leadership is deciding to address problems that everyone knows are present. It is a call to action that involves everyone in the family - the entire crew - all hands.

Given that a *change in responsibility is inevitable* (people are born, marry, and die), our research kept causing us to ask the question concerning whether or not the *preparation for responsibility is so casual and unstructured as to be considered "optional."* The key decision is whether or not to consciously acknowledge that lack of preparation is the single largest risk to transitioning an estate. After that acknowledgement, whether or not the preparation is done well or done poorly is a matter of expertise and commitment. Successful families frequently obtained outside help in the form of a mentor or family coach. The outside (specialized) assistance was in addition to the legal/accounting/financial management help the family had routinely used. They selected a family coach to aid them in their transition planning process. The real skill lies in selecting the appropriate coach for the family's needs.

What are the Critical Attributes of a Competent Family Coach?

Often a family coach is a skilled practitioner who has evolved from another professional field. He or she may have previously been a clinical psychologist, or an estate planner, or even a medical doctor. But all successful coaches will have evolved the following identifiable characteristics:

- They are *not judgmental* or critical. They simply want the best outcome for the family.

- They have developed *a consistent process*, are capable of explaining that process in a manner easily understood.

- They *build skills* with family members in areas necessary for a successful transition of family wealth. They do not stop their work once a solution is found, but instead continue their work until the family is proficient in the skills required to implement and maintain the solution.

- They have a *"track record" of successful families* who are willing to serve as a reference for them and their process.

- *The family feels personally comfortable* and confident when talking with them.

- *The coach is part of a larger team* with a spectrum of resources from which he/she can draw.

The process often requires a team – an assembly of experts in philanthropy, investments, trust and communication, preparing heirs, and mission development. These components all require different skills, and the skills are so critical to the long-term growth and success of a family, that the lead coach cannot be a beginner or minimally competent. The family needs virtuosos and masters, people who are continually designing new processes and techniques, and who are investing in further knowledge in the field; coaches who want to become increasingly skilled in assisting with the breakdowns that occur within families.

How can My Family Select a Family Coach?

When we reviewed the research results, comparing families that successfully transitioned their wealth versus those who did not, certain aptitudes of the family coaches that were used began to surface.

The qualifications listed in the section above were routinely present among the competent family coaches. Successful families had family coaches that emphasized the following aspects of their process:

- *All* family members were interviewed or involved (including spouses and children over age 15) to determine their individual needs.[23]

- *All* family members were included in the family meetings, with the coach present.

- A family wealth mission statement was developed using input from *all* the family members.

- Issues of trust and communications were addressed, and remedies were *practiced* within the family, under the supervision of the coach.

- Issues of the competence[24] required of heirs were discussed and a plan for attaining heir competencies was *installed* and followed.

- The establishment of a mood that welcomed change, accompanied by declarations of "I am a

---

[23] It was effective only if the interviewing was done in person.

[24] Family members need to self-classify with respect to "competence" at a particular task. It was often effective to use verbal equivalents such as "Beginner" or "Novice" with series of progressive (verbal) levels leading to "Expert" or "Master." This enabled members to quantify their personal competence levels without embarrassment. *For Love & Money,* Monterey Pacific Publishing, 1997, pages 102-103

beginner," encouraged family members to learn and grow.

- One outcome of effective coaching was that it was seen as a distinct "plus" by estate planning professionals and financial advisors, and in fact *reduced the costs* of other long-term professional assistance (legal, accounting, etc.).

- Another outcome was that the family understood the role of "accountability" and felt better qualified in *selecting and evaluating professionals* to assist the family in other matters.

The above experiences correlated well with successful family coaches and can be used as "reference questions" that would provide a family with a baseline concerning evaluating a prospective coach. A critical aspect of the above listing confirms that the easier decision to *not* involve the entire family (for scheduling or other reasons) proved consistently harmful to successful family transition planning. Other coach characteristics, such as age, gender, length of time in the field, all seemed to relate more closely to the overall family *comfort level*, especially with the patriarch-matriarch leaders. The three latter factors did not correlate with either success or failure of the family coach.

What are the Signs of a Well-Coached Family?

This is a question a number of families have asked us. They want to visualize their "after" picture as well as their "before" picture. For the most part, our answer was simple. We can recognize a **well-coached family**, with accompanying high odds of a successful wealth transition because:

- There were no "taboo" topics. There were no "dead elephants lying in the living room," which everyone avoided discussing. A well-coached family will talk about anything!

- The family was able to talk, and then take action, even on emotional topics.

- There was a high degree of trust and personal care among/between family members.

- There were open discussions and commitments by all family members regarding promises, requests, and reliability. There was no "pretending" on the level-of-competence scale.

- When breakdowns did occur, discussion and mature dialogue could be heard throughout the entire family.

- They had a clear mission for their wealth, and all could state it accurately.

- Family members were active in the family philanthropies and philanthropy was an integral part of their planning strategy.

- Heirs had a long-range vision of where they fit in the family mission and knew what was expected of them to qualify for any role they chose, as well as the meaning of commitment.

- There was minimal gossip within the family. Most conversations, including criticisms, were open and above board.

- They all understood the tools available, and practiced the skills of communication. They fully appreciated the impact of a promise, and how quickly trust can be betrayed by a broken promise.

SUMMARY: The above are all healthy signs of a well-coached and well-prepared family. Most importantly, they are signs that the heirs are learning (or have learned) how to identify issues, resolve them in a family-friendly manner, and are realists about the levels of competence required to be good stewards of the family's wealth. Well-coached heirs exhibited a remarkable lack of fear, a sense of self-assurance without arrogance or pride, and felt that, together, they can deal with any issue that may confront them or their family. Finally, they appreciated *their strength as a family* and did not see a family of beneficiaries as a burden, but as an opportunity to build together.

7 The Third Step, Preparing The Family's Heirs

Someone needs to listen to the heirs. Often the life of the family centers around managing the family's wealth or business (or businesses), and evolves to reflect the priorities of the patriarch-matriarch. In other words, it is typical that family life begins to be imbalanced around the business of managing assets. Often heirs get "vacuumed into" the business and swept up in daily business responsibilities. Expectations get set, and life for the heirs moves inexorably down a road that no one has discussed with them. Presumptive foundations are laid, and expectations built on those foundations. And the expectations often prove to be grossly incorrect. Heirs begin to feel like a square peg being forced into a round hole.

Our research revealed that a significant percentage of heirs have no desire to be involved in the management of the family assets. College educations may take place far from home, opening the world's borders, establishing new peer relationships, bringing huge changes in the information and opportunities open to heirs. Perhaps an heir falls in love with someone from another country. All the experiences tend to offer heirs alternatives that their parents never had. Today's climate, or culture, encourages less of a sense of "obligation" in younger people. When compounded with a parental (individual) leadership syndrome, the heir begins to believe that there is only need for *one* person to head up the family asset management or family business. Heirs begin to (consciously or unconsciously) defer their involvement to an older or more involved sibling. Alternatively, if the family can get *all* heirs involved in understanding the management of the family assets, and in planning the future, the distinctions between being treated equally versus fairly, or the behavior of deferring to an older sibling is eased. The uninvolved heirs learn about the "sweat equity" (for low pay) that siblings or cousins have invested in the business and, therefore, understand why distributions might be allocated differently. "Everyone being equal" is simply not so when it ignores the differences and interests and experience between heirs involved in the management of family assets/business, and those heirs who are not involved. Conversely, the concept of an older sibling's "sweat equity" being an automatic advantage is also inappropriate.

The goal of successfully transitioning families was to discover the dominant aptitudes and interests in each heir, and to provide each with opportunities to carry forward a *portion* of the family mission. Successful families avoided having the family wealth mission dominate the heir, or become an "unavoidable responsibility" that limited the growth potential of the heir in another direction. Successful families worked hard at accurately matching up heir skills, interests, and competencies with mission and role. That proved effective for the entire family and the health of the estate.

Overlooked Opportunities to Assimilate Family Values Through Involvement in Family Philanthropy

Our research also indicates many missed opportunities for family heirs to be involved in family philanthropy. These opportunities are often unifying and personally fulfilling for the heirs, and are opportunities to learn and test family values. Equally important, philanthropic decision-making involvement begins to teach the heirs early lessons about decisions, money, and accountability. Research on 91 family foundations[25] indicated some remarkable differences in the attitudes of heirs,

---

[25] Roy O. Williams, Prof Newman Peery of U.O.P. Eberhardt School of Business, Private Research entitled "Early Training, Family Foundations and Philanthropic Activity," November 2, 2001

depending on whether or not they were involved early on in the family philanthropy.

Heirs **INVOLVED** in the Family Philanthropy	"If the family loses its wealth, we can earn it back"
Heirs **NOT INVOLVED** in the Family Philanthropy	"Avoid risks for fear of losing the family wealth, because once it's lost, it's gone forever"

The factors behind this surprising difference in attitudes were complex, but seemed to result from the following experiences of the heirs:

1. The heir's values were identified and the heir saw how a family foundation could support those values. (This seemed to set the stage for, "I listen and respect your values, so I expect you to listen and respect my values.")

2. The heir grasped the concept of accountability for decisions that are made concerning money. ("What do you expect your donation to accomplish, and how will you follow up to see that it happens?")

3. The heir applied the concept of remedial action when results varied from expectations. ("If your donation didn't work out, what other

charity might be able to use your donation more effectively? If your donation did work out, should a larger donation be made next year?")

The Wilson family had decided that the five children, ages 12 to 20, should each be responsible for giving $1,000 to a charity of their choice. Each child chose a charity and 13-year old Charlene decided she would give her $1,000 to the Children's Home.

The following year, the family met again to make decisions on their charitable grants. When now 14 year old Charlene was asked if she was going to give to the Children's Home *again*, she said, "No" and told the family that: (1) the Children's Home did not send her a "thank you" note; (2) she went and worked at the home several weekends during the last year and learned her money was used to raise more money and did not go directly to the children in the home. This due diligence set the child, and the family, on an entirely new track.

Today, 25 years later, all the children are good decision makers and perform their due diligence on everything they do. They run the family foundation and have for many years. Their grants are highly effective and the family's values are continually reinforced. Their children have learned how to give, and that money is a *tool*, not a determinant of who they are as individuals.

4. The heir gained an appreciation of the importance of good communication, to let recipients of money know what is expected. ("If you cannot meet my expectations for this contribution, how will you inform me?")

5. The heir developed an understanding of the importance of due diligence in their philanthropic activities, which prepared them for working and living.

The appropriate age for involvement seems to vary, but can begin as early as 12 years old. Early experiments at value-based philanthropy offer the opportunity for the family to praise young heirs for their actions and to reinforce productive philanthropic behavior.

A parent in a wealthy community noticed that his child had set up a lemonade stand in cooperation with a neighbor's child. Pleased with this "spirit of entrepreneurship," he strolled over to congratulate the children. He noticed *two different prices* for lemonade posted on the stand: "50 cents a glass/5 cents a glass" Imagining some sort of "quantity discount" he asked "Why the two prices?" The children happily responded by answering: "Well, the people in our neighborhood can afford to pay 50 cents. But for people outside our neighborhood, 50 cents is too much."

Young people have big hearts, and the lessons here are to give them opportunities to express their values and to talk with them about those values. This is part of preparing heirs to become good stewards, develop their own sense of self-esteem, and let money be a tool, not a definition of who they are.

How can I help my heirs discover their optimum role in life, whatever that may be? There are many assessment tools available. There are many sources of personal help and professional mentoring available. As an heir begins to mature, fairly distinct preferences will evolve. These preferences are not always clearly linked to professional job descriptions. As an example, an heir may express an interest in working for the U.S. Coast Guard at age 16. You and I may hear, "government job, dangerous, drug smugglers, no chance to build the family wealth, always separated from family." What the young person may be thinking is, "service to humanity with a rescue organization, working outdoors, association with a tight group of shipmates." No thoughts about family, or pay, or nearness to siblings.

Next year, the goal may evolve into considering an appointment to the United States Military Academy, until he/she finds out his or her best friend is applying to the University of California at

Santa Cruz because "It has a cool program in oceanography!"

In short, *expect career assessments to change and evolve over time*, and expect that our "mature" sense of the heir's preference may be far from what's in the heir's mind, and far from what is yet to evolve in the heir's mind. Successful families used a range of evaluative and test instruments (questionnaires, interviews, etc.) designed to uncover developing preferences of heirs. The most useful heir interest assessment instruments included the heir's *preferences* for the following:

1. The preferred *type of activity* - physical or mental.

2. The preferred *work setting* – and non-work settings.

3. The types of *colleagues* and interactions desired.

4. The balance between *learning* and simply producing.

5. The desire to *lead* or to follow.

6. The desire for *recognition* and personal achievement.

7. An objective assessment of the heir's current *strengths/weaknesses.*

8. The importance of current *peer groups* and their decisions.

9. The *personality type* of the heir, sources (helping, producing, designing, teaching, etc.) for heir satisfaction.

10. Lastly, *potential career paths* reflective of the heir's preferences in alternatives consistent with 1-9 above.

How do I measure the level of "readiness" of my heirs? The readiness level of heirs to responsibly manage wealth seemed to correlate with the overall readiness of the family itself, with respect to transitioning their wealth and values. The following checklist is informative and covers several of the same areas as the family itself. The text afterwards explains the rationale for the questions.

HEIR READINESS CHECKLIST FOR PARENTS/OWNERS

1. Has a FAMILY WEALTH MISSION been developed with the involvement of the entire family and spouses?
2. Has a STRATEGY to implement the Family Wealth Mission Statement been decided on?
3. Have the ROLES needed to carry out that strategy been defined?
4. Are there specific observable and measurable STANDARDS in place to determine qualifications for each role? - Education - Experience - Family Relationship
5. Has the COMPETENCE LEVEL required for each role been clearly defined (in the range of "Beginner" to "Virtuoso")?
6. Are the heirs and the current family leaders in AGREEMENT on the application of "Standards" and "Competencies" for the defined roles as essential to the success of the Family Wealth Mission?
7. Have heirs selected specific roles and DECLARED THEIR INTEREST in preparing for and serving in those roles?
8. Have conflicts between heirs who may be ASPIRING TO THE SAME ROLE been amicably resolved?
9. Has a specific PROGRAM OF PREPARATION been designed and accepted by heirs designated as candidates for identified roles?
10. Is the program of preparation under way, with agreed-on ALTERNATIVES for each candidate-heir, in the event his/her preparation timetable or completeness for a role is unmet?

The steps outlined above are sufficient to gauge the progress of the preparation level within most inheritance situations. Fully prepared estates will have "YES" answers to all 10 heir checkpoints, greatly reducing the risk of failure in transitioning wealth and values to the heirs. (Recall that 70% of wealth transitions fail.[26]) The preparation of heirs, accompanied by learned skills and *practiced* behavior of communication and trust within the family, are critical to the 30% that succeed. Similar preparation requirements apply whether the heir has a role of financial management oversight (on assets alone), or is expected to oversee some assets of the family enterprise. The above steps are listed in sequential form and can be used as a year-to-year measure of progress.

Question 1. Has a Family Wealth Mission been developed with the participation of the entire family, including the spouses?

This harkens back to the phrase, "Without a declared destination, how do you know if you are going in the right direction?" The question implies the involvement of the heirs, *and the heir's spouse*, in that wealth mission statement and in the communication required to develop that statement. Some organizations currently have formal, detailed

---

[26] MIT, 1983; *"The Economist,"* 6-16-2001

questionnaires focused on the development of a family mission statement. But, while the questions are excellent, those responding to the questionnaire only include the father or mother and do not include the heirs! It is difficult to see how one is able to claim coordination (with respect to the family mission) or heir agreement with the family mission if the heirs are not integral participants in its development.

Question 2. Has a strategy to implement the family wealth mission statement been decided on?

The strategy begins to detail *how* the family will unify behind the agreed-on mission. It also implies that the family is willing to make the sacrifices (in terms of time and income) in order to attain the mission objectives. Finally, once the strategy is agreed on, the tactics, and the roles needed to carry out the tactics, can be decided. Without the strategy agreement, there is likely to be conflict in agreement on methods to be used, roles to be filled, and any sense of unity for the entire transfer of wealth. In addition, objectives and strategy cannot be decided in isolation from others in the family. Everyone's input on strategy must be heard. While there will be disagreement (often strident) early on in strategy discussions, the ability of all voices to get "their two cents in" becomes an important interaction to demonstrate that *everyone* in the family is valuable, important, and worth hearing. Of course, along with listening comes learning and understanding. A final consensus on strategic direction can be evolved sooner (with the assistance of a competent family coach) or later (perhaps never, if the family is unassisted), but the involvement of all is critical to developing family unity leading to a successful wealth transition.

Research indicates that it is always preferable to surface objections or concerns before wealth is transferred than to have those differing views emerge later on, often in the form of lawsuits or disputes. The listening process itself, properly coached, builds skills. It incorporates the general notion of seeking first to understand (the others) and then to be understood (as an individual). This models the (effective) behavior the heir can reasonably expect from siblings and their spouses.

Question 3. Have the ROLES needed to carry out the strategy been defined?

Although roles are identified by strategy, roles are also identified and often constrained by *structure* (i.e. limited partner versus general partner, or foundation trustee versus investment trustee, corporate executive, money manager, investment advisor liaison, real property manager, etc.). In achieving the strategic objectives, it becomes necessary to define the specific roles that need to be filled. Depending on the structure to be served, those roles may range from Director of the Family Foundation to Family Office Executive. The role may be as specific as "Manager of Investment Fund Advisors" or as broad as "Advisor." The roles can be active (president of the family company) or they can be inactive (passive recipient of wealth distributions).

An organization that simply manages wealth (assets) has a substantially different set of roles to be filled than a family that manages a family enterprise (business), plus a foundation, plus a series of trusts, plus a pool of assets. The definition of these roles needs to be done with the entire family's involvement as well as the participation of expert advisors. This is not the moment to assign family members to one role or another. The required competencies and experience have not yet been defined. But now is the time to identify the roles themselves, perhaps to be combined or further subdivided later on. The roles should be defined, standards set to qualify for each role, and the heir's area of responsibility written out for all the family to have on hand as a future (accountability) reference.

Question 4. Are there specific observable and measurable STANDARDS in place to determine qualifications for each role?

- Education
- Experience
- Family Relationship

Once roles are defined, the question becomes one of "How are the occupants of those roles to be measured and evaluated?" The answer to this question lies in the relationship between the complexity of the role, and the importance of the assets under management. As the business or assets grow(s), the roles will become more complex and require new or different skills. The specific preparation for such roles in terms of education, experience, and family relationship will change over time. The family will continually be assessing the heir (accepted for future leadership in that role) to see that preparations are on track, and progress is being made. However, it is much easier if the specifications for that role are observable and measurable: A certain level of educational attainment in a related field/discipline; A certain number of years of work experience at a specified level of responsibility (in terms of money or people, etc.). This makes for clear standards of attainment, and removes charges of "inheriting the job." Of course, failure to meet the specific standards may require an interim period of outside (non-family) assistance from an industry professional who should be held to the same standards of performance.

Situation: Heir "Billy" Rex was asked to vote on decisions involving complex, long-term commercial property exchanges simply because he owned the same percentage of the family estate as the other brothers and sisters. However, Billy was doing a terrific job as a specialty interior designer, and loved his work. He had no interest in real estate, but he did have a vested interest in the family making good real estate decisions.

He felt pressured, inadequate, and unable to do the analysis needed to vote intelligently on important issues involving real estate. He finally told the family that he was "not competent" to make those types of decisions and that he had no intention of reshaping his life to get the education and experience required to become competent. He then asked his younger sister (who had a Masters Degree in real estate finance and was the financial VP of the family corporation) to advise him as to how he should vote. She was comforted by his candor, accepted the added responsibility (which made her even more careful in her analysis), and effectively doubled her voting power in the family enterprise. Everyone felt better, decisions were made more quickly, and harmony ensued.

Failure of the heir to meet the standards within a second "extension period" may require that the role be filled by someone else. Failure to meet the standards may also result in a change in distributions for the heir, perhaps a diversion of funds to a philanthropy of family choosing.

Question 5. Has the COMPETENCE level required for each role been clearly defined?

(We have developed eight levels of defined competence, ranging from "Beginner" to "Master") History is replete with stories of the person who began "in the mailroom" or as a "summer employee" and worked his/her way to the lead of the enterprise. These are examples of the gradual development of various *levels* of competence and a steady broadening of experience.

Competence does not come simply from educational credentials anymore than the experience needed for the VP of finance can come from spending 20 years solely in the mailroom. A clear definition of criteria is required to identify relevant versus irrelevant experience or education.

What is essential is that the family (in participation with its advisors) stake out guidelines for the roles. Those guidelines need to relate performance standards to various competence levels. The guidelines are not etched in stone, but represent generally accepted levels of competence that heirs can clearly comprehend, and work toward, if they wish to play a specific role within the family enterprise.

Recall that the term "enterprise" can be as simple as a pool of liquid assets, or refer to a large (complex) public company where the family has a controlling interest.

Example: The Cavanaugh family decided that any heir having a "significant"* decision-making financial responsibility role within the family enterprise was required to have *at least* a college education *and* five years of "progressively responsible experience" working in a corporation *not* controlled by the Cavanaugh Family.

*The Cavanaugh Family defined "significant" as *"any role capable of obligating more than 1% of the family's liquid assets during a calendar year."*

It makes sense for both the heirs and the family, in general, to *link* the required levels of competence to the responsibility for family assets. It also makes it much easier to decide if a role must be filled immediately, or whether an "outside professional" should fill a role if there are no family members *currently* qualified for the role.

Successful families made durable progress when the requirements for each role has been established, with the assent of the entire family, and the need for competency had not been subverted by expedience. Exceptions that were made (by moving a family member into responsibility before they are *fully* prepared) had special mentoring and/or tutoring accommodations installed for that family member. In short, competent staff needs to surround the heir if the heir is not fully qualified.

Question 6. Are the heirs *and* the current family leaders in agreement on the application of "Standards" and "Competencies" for the defined roles as essential to the success of the Family Wealth Mission?

This question is directed at avoiding any "bullying" by the current family leadership, and to remind the leadership that family assent *and* support is critical to family harmony following the transfer of wealth and responsibility. It is understood that standards may change as the marketplace changes, as technology changes, and as the structure of the enterprise changes. The family enterprise may decide to make a major foray overseas - or decide to license new products or services - or liquidate part of the business and require a skill shift to liquid asset management (as opposed to company operating managers). These types of changes may require new competencies, thus automatically selecting (or deselecting) another family member with previously less-valued (and perhaps less relevant in the past) competencies.

The heart of this question goes back to reaching agreement on evaluating the performance of the heir. It is, at its roots, a matter of the family's willingness to do the hard work to *objectively* measure the performance of other family members with family wealth responsibilities, and for heirs to be willing to be held accountable for performance. Agreement by the entire family on standards and competencies leads to acceptance of the concept of performance measurement and accountability for any, and every, family member or spouse. This brings certainty, predictability, and stability to the entire family.

Question 7. Have the heirs selected specific roles and declared their interest in preparing for, and serving in, those roles?

Be concerned about the heir who accepts any responsibility thrust on her/him. A healthier outlook is for the heir to be able to engage the family leadership in a "Why me?" conversation. Healthier yet, is the family who understands the skills and interests of the heir and communicates their encouragement and continued support to the heir who knowledgeably accepts the new responsibilities. Simply to have the heir say, "I'll do it" (without full and complete discussion) is neither fair to the heir, nor fair to the family.

There are a series of steps that should be taken to confirm the heir's basic interests, assess heir skills and competencies, and discuss the heir's willingness to obtain additional training and experience for the role being considered. What the family should seek, on behalf of the heir, *is a good match*. Careful assessment of the role's needs, by itself, is *not* sufficient. Even if the heir is found to be "able to perform," *that is not sufficient.* The heir may be able to function in the role at a "minimally competent" skill level. Much more learning may be required to move to a "proficient" level. [27]

What families should seek from the heir is the sincere expression of interest in the role. A "sincere" expression of interest means that the heir:

1. Completely understands the role and the standards for performing the role competently.

2. Has an appreciation and affinity for the role.

3. Is likely to find personal fulfillment and happiness in preparing for the role and in filling the role.

---

[27] Ibid, footnote 21

Without those three criteria, it is unlikely an heir can make a *sincere* declaration of interest in the role, or carry out the sustained level of learning and experience to qualify for that role.

Question 8. Have conflicts between heirs, who may be aspiring to the same role, been amicably resolved?

What happens when *all* heirs want to be the future CEO of the family enterprise? What happens when two heirs want to be Vice President for Marketing? How do issues get resolved if there is a conflict in the individual heirs' goals?

One must take care here to not "shut down" or prematurely select one heir at the price of alienating or losing the involvement of the other heir. It is a delicate moment many families have slowly worked their way through using the passage of time and patience.

If the discussion can be well grounded by using observable, measurable family standards (and levels of competence), then the rival siblings/heirs will usually reach the same conclusion as to who is most qualified and has affinity for the role.

The two themes of "careful analysis" and "open discussion" - *with the use of outside assistance* - seems to have inevitably resolved intra-heir conflicts revolving around asset management roles. With the notion of "family teamwork" established, with agreement on the family's wealth mission, and with the skills at communication in full operation, a solid foundation exists to resolve such conflicts.

An openly competing set of wishes, declared by the heirs, is much healthier for the family than concealed competitive behavior. In general, the patriarch-matriarch needs to embrace the concept of heirs striving or competing for a position in managing the family wealth. The problem of competing for a future role is much more manageable than either:

1. Concealed competition or,

2. Fear and loathing about being involved in the management and responsibility of the family wealth.

Of all the problems that a patriarch/matriarch faced, that of sorting out *which* heir was destined for *which* role was one problem that benefited most from outside assistance and coaching. Issues surrounding, "It was Dad's decision," or, "I knew Mom was going to side with you, she always does!" were reframed in an atmosphere of "What's best for the family?" That reframing seemed to be most effective when done with an "outside" family-coaching professional.

The Martell family built a $200 million company, educated their sons at the best universities, with both attending first-rate business schools. Competitively encouraged, the sons were always trying to out-perform one another. This competitive behavior carried through to auto purchases, to home building, and to managing sectors of the family company. The parents hired consultants to mediate between the brothers, brought in University Family Business Management Centers, and even hired two retired judges from the Superior Court to mediate their behavior. The behavior was becoming destructive to the family company, threatening its financial stability, and was severely hurting their relationship as a family.

A competent family coach was brought in, interviewed the family members and their spouses, and then began a series of family meetings. The family realized that the source of the problem was parental encouragement of competitive behavior. Parents changed patterns of reward and recognition, restored communication, rebuilt trust, and the sons ceased competing with one another in an unhealthy manner.

Heirs do need to actively participate in the *process* of resolving their competition for a future role. The resolution answer emerges from a closer examination of the heirs' motivation, interest levels, competencies, and time necessary before the heirs' full preparation (for the role) is attained.

This means the outside coach must enter into further in-depth conversations with the heirs, involve them in three-way discussions about the role and its requirements, and simultaneously assess other (vacant?) family mission roles that might benefit (from) their skills. This process may take months, involving 30-day spans between one-day meetings with the competing heirs and the outside coach.

In the end, it must be the heirs' joint responsibility to announce their "findings" (the suggested resolution) to the entire family at a family meeting. They need to make that announcement personally, together, in order to:

- Model the required behaviors on how conflict within the family is resolved

- Reinforce the notion that they are part of a family team

- Demonstrate that family wealth disputes get resolved for the greater good of the family.

If properly handled, this is simply another "bump in the road" that presents an effective opportunity to learn, teach, and strengthen the family.

Question 9. Has a specific program of preparation been designed and accepted by heirs designated as candidates for identified roles?

Preparing heirs for future roles cannot be a general notion - it must deal with specifics. If it deals with educational preparation, the questions need to focus on what educational degree, in what time frame? If not with formal education, it needs to define what alternative learning is required, from where, and how it is to be measured. Is formal licensure or admittance to the profession required? Is there a requirement for maintenance of licensure or certification as part of the learning for the role to be taken in the family wealth management? And who foots the bill for further education, or practice classes for professional certification exams? If the goal is to prepare for a family responsibility role, then clearly the family should foot the bill. Perhaps the payment for further education or training (including a living allowance until completion) is "forgiven" at a rate of 20% per year of employment within the family enterprise.

Your professional advisors will have many mechanisms to handle these situations, but the agreement on the program to prepare the heir *must ultimately be between the family and the heir.* Successful transition families did not let the financial managers, accountants, or lawyers decide on a development program for the heir. Those families did not see this development program for the heir as a legal, tax, or financial decision. It was seen as a family communication and commitment discussion – after which the legal and tax people were notified and provided the structure required to implement what the family wanted.

These specifics of development should be detailed in a "contract" between the patriarch/matriarch and the heir, including what the heir might expect if he/she falls short on any of the specifics. This same contract should define what levels of experience (demonstrating growth in operating skill) are needed. Is it "five years of steadily advancing responsibility as an investment advisor with earnings (plus incentives), increasing by no less than 10% each year?" Is the experience to be gained in a corporate environment, in an industry similar to that of the heir's family business, or experience abroad? Or, is it experience in a functional department such as sales or finance? It is important that changes to the contract/agreement should occur only when *both* parties consent to such changes. Changes might be required by a death in

130

the family, or the sale of a division, or a change in the market, or circumstances surrounding the family enterprise. But, changes to the program of preparation should be made carefully, and then only after thoughtful consideration and acceptance by the patriarch/matriarch and the heir involved.

> Tom Gannon sat down and spoke privately with the family coach he had brought in to help. Tom confessed that he was "afraid" for the first time in his life. When the coach inquired why, Tom said, "My Dad is 80 years old, and he just told me that I am taking over as president of our billion dollar family business in January. I've worked for Dad all my life, and he's never allowed me to fail. I don't know if it is because he would have been embarrassed, or because he wanted to protect me. Now, for the first time in my life, I am going to be allowed to fail...and I'm scared to death!"

It is clearly more meaningful to allow heirs to learn, and have "small" failures, rather than to "protect" them over time, suddenly saddling them with the major and unrelenting responsibility of leadership. It is not a favor to heirs to protect them from failure. It conceals weakness. It reduces learning. It fails to teach them how to deal with risk and failure. It artificially makes them think perfection is the measure. These are serious mistakes, done in the name of love for the children.

Question 10. Is the program of preparation underway, with agreed on alternatives for each candidate-heir, in the event his or her preparation timetable or completeness for a role is unmet?

It is important to get a program of preparation underway if it is not already in effect. Courses, specialty instruction, tutoring, and other vehicles can get the formal preparation jump-started while the conversations are fresh and the passion is still high. Reinforce the elements[28] of the "contract" for heir preparation by initiating action, announcing the process is underway, and do it as soon as possible. The family should be prepared to financially support such preparation, whether in the form of tuition, fees, study, etc. It is, in fact, preparation for the benefit of the family.

The difficulty arises when the heir "falls off the (preparation) wagon." What happens then? If the derailment is a simple setback, and easily remedied in a short time, the patriarch/matriarch should be generous in understanding, encouraging the heir to get back on course as soon as possible. *The slip should not be ignored.* It must be discussed with the heir. It may be a symptom of unreliability. A more

---

[28] Elements consist of specifics (including timetables) for measurable and observable preparatory characteristics such as the level of knowledge, amount of experience, demonstration of abilities, and the proof of performance in progressively relevant assignments (inside or outside the family business).

serious derailment *may* require that interim people be hired (even from the outside) to fill the role until the heir has met the preparation requirements.

During the first meeting with the Chanya family, the oldest heir, Tary, asked why he should get a job. "What's the purpose? Grandfather left me $10 million in stock, and I'm receiving about $900,000 each year. Like, what's the reason for working? I don't get it."

After several meetings, Tary began to realize that issues of dignity, competence, self-reliance, and self-esteem were wrapped up in decisions he needed to make *separately* from his grandfather's bequest. He declared himself "a beginner" and set out on a course to pursue a lifelong interest in ecological water quality issues. With the help of a mentor, he worked diligently, prepared himself carefully, and eventually headed up a successful company - to the unending pride of his parents.

Finally, if it is a serious setback, and the reasons for the setback signify that the heir is *not* likely to resume an agreed-on preparation course, then a recharting of the heir's preparation is required. The setback, or delay, may have nothing to do with the heir's competence, reliability, or sincerity - and little to do with clear business issues. A range of circumstances (the inability of a role to engage the heir's giftedness, a change of life priorities, health issues, etc.) could necessitate a revision to the agreement with the heir, leading to preparation for a different role. This may be an agreement to delay the placement of the heir into the agreed-on role *until* some additional requirements are met. Or, this may require the coach be recalled to reanalyze the situation, meet with the heir, and reset some targets and preparation plans.

Heirs may get married, or twins may be born, or a friend may have a severe time of need. The roles needed within the corporation may change with time and the marketplace. If the heir values the strength of good relationships, and has to take time out to respond to the needs of those relationships, then that's a good indication that the proper values are in place. If, however, the heir falls short of the preparation timetable that he/she has agreed to, and does not wish to be held accountable for the slip, then the link to "family role" is broken. In some cases, we have seen heirs take an adult "time out" and return to school, or travel, or gain some valuable work experience in an unrelated field, only to resume preparation at a later date. One cannot prepare (contract) for all eventualities and all forces that are likely to tug an heir off course. However, one can hold the heir accountable for the timetable and preparation that was *within the heir's control* to which the *heir agreed*. Failure to act on the heir's preparation failures will only lead to more failures.

SCORING: The "Heir Readiness Checklist" is approximately sequential. All 10 questions should ultimately be answered, "Yes." Those estates which have heirs with the ability to answer all 10 questions, "Yes" will have minimized the risk of failure in transitioning their wealth. Recall that is not simply the "knowing" that is critical, it is the conversion of knowledge into action ("doing") that offsets the risk that heirs will be damaged, or might lead the family estate to ultimate failure. For that reason, the above checklist carries with it a presumption that the family works on (and maintains) a high level of trust and communication within the family, keeps updating and referencing the family wealth mission, and closely follows the preparation course of action being followed by the heir(s). Only with that close attention to preparing heirs for wealth with responsibility can the family move its estate from the "likely to fail" group into the "likely to succeed" group.

8 The Fourth Step, The Heir's Self-Preparation Responsibilities

Throughout this book we have been communicating what successful families have done to ensure successful transition of the family's values and wealth, with emphasis on the responsibilities of the patriarch/matriarch. The establishment and maintenance of trust and communication within the family, and a program to define the mission/strategy and roles to carry out the mission are foundational. We have also provided the patriarch/matriarch with a checklist to determine heir readiness in the previous chapter.

Throughout the research and in 39 years of experience with family leaders, we continually heard the question asked: "I know what I need to do, and what the family needs to do, but what responsibilities does the heir have?" "Is it all on *our* shoulders?" This chapter responds to that question and lays out the self-examination heirs of successful wealth transition families have gone through.

Successful families realized at some point that simply building and preserving wealth was not a satisfying goal, nor was it reflective of their personal hopes for their children. They came to focus on wealth being an "enabler" for their heirs, as opposed to being a "burden" to their heirs. As these successful families increased their emphasis on family wealth as a vehicle to create opportunities for their children (beyond retaining and building the wealth itself), they expanded the opportunities for their heirs. The major concerns of successful families became a simple sequence of:

1. Determining what the "giftedness" was for each heir and how, individually, they were unique in their motivation

2. Making each heir aware that the family wanted them to realize their fullest self-potential

3. Developing a process, within and involving the entire family, to help those heirs achieve their dreams

4. Accepting that world events will cause bumps in the road, change, disruption, and that the family is there to help one another learn from (and live through) those "bumps."

Heirs, therefore, played a critical and intimately involved role in determining their own future alignment with the family values and wealth. From these successful families, we have distilled their internal processes into the form of a **"Readiness Self-Checklist for Heirs."** In many ways it is the counterpoint to the family leadership checklist for preparing heirs. The 10 most important checkpoints they used are summarized on the following page.

READINESS SELF-CHECKLIST FOR HEIRS

1.	Have I worked with my parent(s) and other family members to define a clear long-term MISSION for the family wealth?
2.	Have I actively worked with my family to develop the STRATEGY for achieving the mission of the family wealth?
3.	Have the various ROLES for the management of the family assets been identified, and do I support filling those ROLES with fully competent individuals?
4.	Do I know what my PERSONAL INTERESTS are, and understand my ABILITIES well enough to identify a specific role for myself?
5.	In preparing for a particular role, am I willing to be evaluated against specific observable and measurable STANDARDS? • Education (formal and informal) • Experience (task, competitive, charitable) • Family Relationships (building, strengthening)
6.	Have I selected a MENTOR whom I respect, who cares about my personal fulfillment, but who will be honest with me with respect to my contributions to the family mission?
7.	Have I developed, with my Mentor, a specific plan to become COMPETENT for the family mission role that satisfies my interests and talents, within the mission staffing timeframe?
8.	Am I EMOTIONALLY OPEN to the communications requirements and the continuing learning and evaluation that is required of each role-occupying individual within the family wealth mission structure?
9.	Do I clearly understand the difference between KNOWING (what needs to be done) versus DOING (what needs to be done) and to discipline myself to act in the best interests of the mission?
10.	Have I assumed personal responsibility for learning from the unavoidable "BUMPS IN THE ROAD" as demonstrated by developing (and maintaining) the skills to strengthen my family during difficult times?

Question 1. Have I worked with my parent(s) and other family members to define a clear, long-term MISSION for the family wealth?

This is the counterpart to the question given to the entire family, and places personal responsibility on the shoulders of the heir to participate, cooperate, clarify, and reach ultimate agreement in support of a family wealth mission statement. Asking the question about working "with parents and other family members" stresses the importance of whole family involvement, and of communication skills, and probes the heir's agreement with declaration of the family wealth mission.

Question 2. Have I actively worked with my family to develop the strategy for achieving the mission of the family wealth?

The important word here is "actively." Working with the family (and their professional outside coaches) to formulate the strategy for achieving the mission requires involvement, thought, and sets the foundations for what will be required to achieve that mission. It forces the heir to come up with specifics, and to think through the use of observable, measurable standards for evaluating the attainment of mission. This will prepare the heir for a discussion on roles to attain the family mission, not his/her personal mission. It also removes a sense of detachment or separateness from the family mission.

Question 3. Have the various roles for the management of the family assets been identified, and do I support filling those roles with fully competent individuals?

This is the counterpoint that puts the heir on the spot by asking about his/her personal commitment to "competence" as the basis for selection. It presumes that the family has progressed towards identifying roles, and now asks the heir to declare himself/herself as to whether or not *the family is entitled to competent individuals* in those roles. The unacceptable alternative is the concept of "entitlement" to a job because the family owns the company or assets under management. The adverb "fully" refers to a preparation level that is toward the "master" end of the scale, and not toward the "beginner" end. It clearly asks for a declaration as to whether or not the heir supports the preparation required to become "fully competent." To do this requires the heir to declare publicly himself/herself to be a "beginner."

Frequently, we have encountered entrepreneurs who sold their company, or exercised stock options and found themselves with a pile of cash. They uniformly felt that because they were good managers of people and processes, they must also be good at managing their money (liquid assets). They could not ground this belief with any evidence of competence or experience in money management. In fact, the opposite was true. They did not have the risk profile for money management, and could only be categorized as pre-beginners or "pretenders" at best.

One graduate of a prominent business school had a 6-inch spindle of unreturned phone messages on her desk as *The Williams Group* Coach was interviewing her. When the coach asked about the work habits behind unreturned phone calls, the President of the company replied:

"I just sold a bunch of my stock for $22 million. I am ashamed to say that I don't know how to manage cash... but I do know how to manage my company! So, I had my secretary open up FDIC insured accounts in my name for $100,000 each - in 220 different accounts. All those calls are asking if I want to roll over the CDs. At least I won't lose anything!"

Unwilling to declare herself a "beginner," and too embarrassed to ask for help at a task that she felt an MBA and CEO *should* know how to do, she was now seeking help from a professional coach. Over a period of six months she learned how to select money managers, and how to hold them accountable for her fund performance - and returned her attention to running her company.

Most lost a lot of money before they accepted guidance from a skilled practitioner in the field of asset management.

Question 4. Do I know what my personal interests are and understand my abilities well enough to identify a specific role for myself?

This really asks three questions of the heir: Do I know myself and my interests? And, do I know my abilities at this point in my life? It asks the heir's preparation and willingness to learn. "Can I declare myself a 'beginner'? is an evaluative question designed to encourage the heir to cooperate with the family leadership (and a family coach) in determining the steps necessary to prepare for a future role. The heir, at this point, may have targeted several roles in which he/she might be interested... yet not know the specific differences between marketing, sales, advertising and public relations as it affects the family wealth. At the early stages, simply knowing one's interests and abilities, objectively and honestly, is sufficient to respond well to the professional coach's efforts to develop a career plan. Successful families worked hard at having the heir declare their personal interests in order to select long-term roles that would be a solid match.

Question 5. In preparing for a particular role, am I willing to be evaluated against specific observable and measurable STANDARDS?

- Education (formal and informal)
- Experience (task, competitive, charitable)
- Family Relationships (building, strengthening)

Here the heir is being asked to accept that there are educational, experiential, and family relationship requirements for every role. Beyond the earlier questionnaire, it is a reminder of the need to discuss formal and informal educational and experience requirements, and defines family relationships as "building and strengthening." At this point, it would be difficult for an heir to fall into a major dispute with the family about the need for a careful program of preparation if, in fact, the heir wishes to play a role in the management of the family wealth. The foundations are logical, and historically have proven to be compelling from the data we have collected. On the other hand, there may be no role in the management of the families' assets that is a good match for the heir's giftedness or interests. Nonetheless, the process remains useful for the heir that seeks alternatives outside the family.

Question 6. Have I selected a mentor whom I respect, who cares about my personal fulfillment, but who will be honest with me with respect to my contributions to the family mission?

Here we imply the requirements of shared respect between the heir and the mentor, a concern for the personal well being of the heir, and complete honesty (and often, complete confidentiality) with respect to whether or not the heir is "making the grade" in preparing for and supporting the family mission. Important to this process is personal evaluation as to the heir's level of competence, which the coach/mentor should be continually assessing.

The mentor should not be a peer of the heir, and should not be selected on the basis of friendship. The mentor should be older than the heir and certainly more experienced, while also being skilled at drawing the heir into the self analysis and objectivity needed to accurately understand the heir's progress toward competence. The self-esteem of the heir should be the mentor's first concern, with the understanding that self-esteem can only arise from thoughtful preparation, overcoming obstacles, and being recognized as a contributor to the family mission. Of course, this same growth in self-esteem can come from the heir's acknowledged performance in a non-family environment as well.

Competence developed by the heir will lead to confidence. Confidence inevitably leads to self-esteem. It is a positive reinforcement sequence.

A reminder here might be in order: the heir must have been actively involved in the development of the mission for the family and its wealth. There should be no question of the heir's support for the family mission. If there is some doubt about the heir's support, that is the first aspect that needs to be addressed with the mentor, since it might be evidence of insincerity, a lack of comprehension, non-participation, or simply of an attempt to "go along." Mentors are tutors. Mentors are active counselors who are paid from the family wealth, *but who are responsible to the heir, not the family.*

The mentoring process in successful families was always initiated following an extensive initial interview with the heir. [29] This provided the mentor with a deeper understanding of the environment and the relationships. Thenceforth, the contact between the mentor and the heir was both scheduled (progress evaluations) and episodic in response to a need of the heir ("I have a question," or, "A change has occurred").

---

[29] A series of interviews with other family members and spouses had previously been performed developing the family wealth mission statement.

Mentoring usually continues for one to three years, and sometimes as long as 10 or 20 years. As time passes, the relationship and the bond between the mentor and heir can deepen, but it is consistently important that the mentor remain professionally uninvolved with the family assets. No confusion should be allowed between the mentor's obligation to the heir, and the priority of the heir being compromised by any obligation that could be presented by the mentor's involvement with the family's assets. The family has entrusted their most valuable asset to the mentor: their heir.

Question 8. Am I emotionally open to the communications requirements and the continuing learning and evaluation required of each role-occupying individual within the family wealth mission structure?

It is one thing to say one is open to the communication requirements, and another thing to actually accept that the communication is a requirement and believe in its power ("emotionally open"). The foundation of mutual intra-family trust is built on the three pivot points of reliability, sincerity, and competence. The continuation of that trust cannot be sustained without honest, open, and transparent communications. No duplicity. No "spinning." No guile. No manipulation. Just the honest truth, so that the family can take mutual action in a coordinated fashion - action they understand, support, and are united by with respect to accepting/sharing responsibility for the outcome. Each role-occupying heir has this responsibility.

The other two components, "continuing learning" and "evaluation," ask the heir to understand that the learning doesn't end when the heir is assigned to the role. Earning the role does not promise keeping the role. Continued learning and the development of skills necessary for the role are the expectation of successful families - just as they would expect from any professional (non-family) "outside" occupant of that role.

The measurement of the continuing learning, and competence in the role, is involved in the term "evaluation." The heir needs to understand and accept that being evaluated is a part of the role. The evaluation is formal as well as informal. It involves performance of the responsibility (e.g., return on investment >12%) and application of the family values (e.g., "We do not lie, cheat, steal, or take advantage of others in unfortunate situations."). These are the all important antecedents needed to establish trust (reliability, sincerity, competence). Evaluation is the necessary feedback that indicates what needs to be learned, what needs to be changed, and needs to be achieved by the next evaluation point. The heir must acknowledge and fully embrace all elements of Question 8.

Question 9. Do I clearly understand the difference between knowing (what needs to be done) versus doing (what needs to be done) and to discipline myself to act in the best interests of the mission?

Seldom do failures occur because we didn't *know* what to do. The failures occur because we didn't act in a timely fashion to convert what we *know* into what we *do*. Our research repeatedly showed that family leaders (parents) knew what needed to be done to balance their time at the business with their time at the family, but that they consistently failed to take the actions required to achieve that balance. It wasn't as if they didn't know. They knew, and yet they persisted in staying "out of balance" between work and family, and their family/heirs/harmony and transition paid the price for it.

Curiously, parents want to avoid that same imbalance in their children (heirs). The heir needs to develop the balancing skills necessary for his/her upcoming role, and then needs to understand that he/she will be evaluated on *how he/she has put those learned skills into practice*, not simply on what skills he/she has "learned." The learned skills benefit the family only if they are applied effectively. It is this conversion of knowledge into action that is one of the more difficult tasks for an heir to learn. In part, it is a fear of failure that causes the hesitancy of the heir to act. In short, it involves learning how to deal with the unavoidable failures, as well as the occasionally unearned successes. It involves learning how to recover. And it involves moving on to the next challenge, armed with an understanding of the causes of failure/success, and a desire to avoid the same mistake again.

Surprisingly, research has shown that children who, early in life, were given the opportunity to make recommendations to the family foundation were recognized with a grant to their favorite charity.

Yet, many times, when the family urged the child to "follow-up" and be sure the grant benefited what (or whom) it was intended for, the child sometimes experienced one of his or her first disappointments with financial managers. This experience had taught them the importance of accountability. Having "failed" in their first grant, the children then became much more penetrating in their questions—before making their second grant—often changing their administering charity. (This activity provides hand-on experiences in "continuing learning", "analyzing the causes of failure", and "taking corrective action.")

Life teaches us that the second-best plan, well executed, will inevitably beat a superior plan that is poorly executed. That is the lesson of correctly converting knowledge into action.

Question 10. Have I assumed personal responsibility for learning from the unavoidable "bumps in the road" as demonstrated by developing (and maintaining) the skills to strengthen my family during difficult times?

The heir's self-preparation concludes with this question of "personal responsibility" for learning, improving, and using both skills to strengthen the family. Not just strengthening the family assets, but strengthening the *family itself*. Successful families and their heirs and spouses learned and practiced how to overcome perceived betrayal or old hurts, and thereby were able to address trust issues. Big losses and mistakes were overcome and used as learning points. There is no permanent fix for trust. Trust needs to be maintained and repaired when it has been broken. It is simply *normal* that breaches of trust will occur in any large family. What is critical is that the family has learned how to move on and grow as they individually exercise their learned skills at repairing and restoring trust.

One of our early pieces of research looked at the difference between families that valued *assets* first, and those that valued *family* first. We encountered wealthy families where the family leader simply declared that the company "was not a parking lot for family members." That was an attempt to require competence, rather than a purposeful exclusion of family members from working in the family company. Thus everyone, who wanted to be in the family business had to earn their way in and prove their competence. In our research, the successful wealth transitions considered family unity equally important to family financial strength.[30] Their family life and family interactions were "in balance" with their income-generating responsibilities. "Bumps in the road," the phrase used within the checklist, refers to the inevitable reversals and conflicts that arise in the normal course of living. New automobile designs are not tested solely on the racetrack. They are tested (evaluated) by how the designs respond to "bumps in the road," including their response to the unexpected. The operating envelope for the vehicle is pushed outward by test drivers and engineers so that the design becomes "inherently forgiving" for the average driver. It is from the more severe tests (the most severe "bumps in the road") that the

---

[30] Chapter 5, question #9

engineers and designers *learn to build the better car.* Therefore, it is from the more severe tests of the heir that the heir learns to strengthen his or her family. That is what is being asked with this question.

SCORING: The steps outlined above are basic to gauging an heir's personal progress in preparing for the responsibility of wealth. Fully prepared heirs will have "YES" answers to all checklist items, and the heir's mentor will be in agreement with those scores. This greatly reduces the risk of failure in preparing for and assuming responsibilities for family wealth and values. The worldwide data is incontrovertible - 70% of wealth transitions will fail.[31] The careful preparation of heirs, accompanied by *learned* skills and *practiced* behavior of communications and trust within the family are critical to the 30% that succeed.

These generalized preparation questions are valid whether the heir has a role in financial management, financial management oversight, or is actively working in the family enterprise itself, including the family foundation. The above steps are listed in somewhat sequential form and can be used as a year-to-year measurement of progress.

---

[31] MIT, 1983; *"The Economist,"* 6-16-2001

9 The Fifth Step, Continuing Evaluation and Measurement

Anyone who believes that they can manage money for others without acknowledging that they will be evaluated and measured themselves is simply not dealing with reality. It isn't any less forgiving just because it is your own family money. It is true that some major executives go quite a while using "OPM" (Other People's Money) before they are held accountable. Some even make it to their graves having never been called to task. But in a wealthy family, where the heir anticipates stewardship for some part of the family wealth, and others are depending on that stewardship, the heir should expect accountability! Once again, the quicksand is a shortfall in communication and trust. Normal setbacks, or "bumps in the road" as families often refer to them, are frequently seen as abnormal by uninformed and uneducated family members. Following an unexpectedly poor performance, an heir/steward may not even be allowed an explanation if the family lacks communication and trust habits with respect to the management of their wealth. Without every family member assuming that "best efforts" are the motivation of "fully competent" leader-heirs (or their selected professionals), family leadership can become a recurring litany of gossip, accusations, and simple misinformed anger. Remember, trust is a sacred gift we give to others (and they to us). Trust takes a long time to build and can be broken in an instant. Yet breaks in trust are inevitable. The critical issues are: have the skills to rebuild and repair trust been acquired, and are they in practice within the family?

There are no shortcuts for communicating with the rest of the family. In the absence of information, people fill that vacuum with their worst fears and suspicions. This leads to gossip, and gossip kills the atmosphere of trust within the family because it shuts off open communication. The communication skills of heirs can be blunted by the example of parents who operate under the mode of "I make the decisions around here." If that is what the heir learns as the acceptable manner of communicating, the heir will not be encouraged to become more open with his/her communication.

A family ownership is a much more critical environment even than publicly owned companies with their regulatory reporting requirements. The family company shareholder/owner group is smaller and more intimate. People within that group tend to be in easy communication, and they all share a history, which few public shareholder groups can claim. They also tend to react more like a school of geese, flying in gaggles and individual groups, separate, yet all heading toward the same overall destination. These are not public shareholders and not diversified in their investments. A subgroup within a family can reach an agreement or an opinion (for good or ill) overnight. Accordingly, the following principles must be kept uppermost in the managing heir's thoughts:

- **Uninformed owners** (fellow heirs and their spouses/families) are likely to make grievous assumptions about any downward changes in their distributions or asset values.

- **Non-participating heirs** cannot be supportive and cannot offer constructive criticism if they do not know what's going on.

- **Heirs unschooled in business or asset management**, and the marketplace they operate within, are unable to experience valuable "bumps in the road." They don't learn how to assess negative experiences, or how to recover/adapt.

The Maze family of 15 heirs was dependent on the family company for the support of their lifestyle. While they had come to expect annual payouts in the $300,000 range, they had never taken the time to understand the business and the three managing heirs were simply too busy to "tutor" the family members. In late 2001, the individual distributions were cut to $150,000 for the first time. The non-managing family was furious, promptly banded together, forced the resignation of the 3 managing heirs, and brought in professional managers. The professional managers reported: at the end of their first 90 days, the 3 managing heirs "managed to make money while all their competitors were losing money, increased the company's market share by 15 percentage points, and saw their largest competitor filing for bankruptcy-possibly increasing the Maze's market share *another* 20% in the next 60 days!"

The Maze family realized they had acted hastily, without full knowledge, and asked the 3 managing heirs to return to the leadership of the family business. The managing heirs declined, announced they had decided to go into business for themselves, and were filing a lawsuit to force the family company to buy them out because they needed the funds to begin their own business. Unable to borrow, the Maze Company had to sell their flagship division to raise the funds, and the following year the distributions were cut to $50,000 instead of returning to the scheduled $300,000 level.

- **If the managing heir evades accountability**, the stage is set for the next managing heir to behave in a similar fashion, with recurring destructive consequences for the family wealth and unity.

The American landscape is liberally sprinkled with fictionalized movie and book characters who purvey the false image of the "Savior Soldier" or "Lonesome Cowboy," who comes to individually rescue the suffering masses. Movies dwell on the Lone Ranger theme and announcers look for the "Player of the Game." The truth is, most successful achievements of almost any significance are the result of inspired, unified, and closely-knit *teams*. Most of those teams respond to a shared mission, and follow a leader who represents and coheres to their highest hopes and dreams. John Wayne didn't really save the West. Audie Murphy didn't really win WWII. Thomas Edison alone didn't really invent the light bulb. And Caesar didn't really build Rome, *alone*. The ability to attain individual "heroism" is a false measure of any heir's competence.

The Upcoming Heirs: Finally, heirs need to be measured on whether or not they have commenced planning responsibilities for the family wealth into the next generation - perhaps the heir's children or the children of a sibling, or perhaps even the spouse of a direct heir. The goal is to do what is best for the family, and to maintain the balance between family unity and financial strength. *That cannot be done in isolation.* The data indicates deciding alone is a very bad bet, and is likely to precipitate failures.

Balance and successful transition may require outside professional management to fill some roles where a family member is neither interested nor competent. The strategic roles may have shifted. The managing heir's skills of running the *family real estate* may have to be modified/retrained the heir in a new set of skills needed to manage the *purely financial assets* that replace the now-sold real estate. Installing a process of *continuing evaluation and measurement* for upcoming heirs is basic to any well-run enterprise, and it is no different for family leadership.[32] The managing heir/steward needs to accept responsibility for modeling (actually behaving) his/her personal acceptance of being measured and evaluated. That is the most convincing (and permanent) modeling for upcoming heirs over the longer term. The heir that is prepared for responsibility by understanding and accepting the measurement process is well positioned to carry through a smooth and

---

[32] Successful families often elected an "Executive Committee" to represent the family interests between annual family meetings. These Executive Committees were, in turn, held accountable to the family-wide ownership and served as a sort of "buffer" between the family and the family CEO.

successful transition of the family wealth, the family values, and the accompanying family unity.

Outside Resources on Standby: Professional advisors in the fields of heir preparation, financial management, estate planning, accounting, operations management, and specialized consulting firms represent major sources of assistance. When an heir's preparation or interest lags, or when performance is not up to par, it is time to call on the outside resources for assistance. Often the opportunity for an heir to take a "breather" in preparation for family wealth management responsibilities enables the heir to avoid discouraging failures before the heir is ready. In addition, the "breather" may offer a natural opportunity to commence a mentor relationship as the professional (interim) help steps into the heir's role. The gradual departure of the professional can smoothly transition responsibilities to the now-prepared heir, serving as a source of counsel and advice. Succession planning is a requirement for family enterprises, as well as publicly held enterprises.

Most businesses, *large or small*, public or private, get 40 to 80 hours of weekly attention from their CEO or managing director. The size of the business determines the size of the problem that the CEO focuses on (not the total amount of attention, because that is finite). The CEO of one major corporation took years grooming three major potential successors for the position of CEO. When he finally announced his selection, the other two candidates promptly left to head up other Fortune 500 companies. In the final measure, the (parent) CEO (or heir/steward) is responsible for evaluating people (managers and heirs) with respect to their progress toward a strategic objective: evaluating people. For that reason, the identification, development, and selection of competent heirs remains the major *transitional responsibility* of the managing heir or parent, and they need to be held accountable for progress in that area.

10 Closing Observations and Summary

Conclusions and recap: The research data leads to conclusions that are undeniable. The odds of a successful wealth transition are about 30%. These are terrible odds. *The Williams Group* studied data from 3,250 families that transitioned their wealth to analyze why, although some succeeded in the transition, the majority failed. Thousands of direct interviews were conducted, and it was discovered that less than 3% of the failures were attributed to poor professional help. Consider that: less than 3% of estate transition failures were caused by poor tax decisions, inadequately prepared legal documents, faulty accounting or records, etc. This is evidence that the legal and tax professional community have a solid grasp of their jobs in wealth transition! That professional community's focus on the issues of taxation, preservation, and governance is well honed, well understood, and well performed.

The causes for wealth transition failure: 70% of wealth transitions fail. The most important single issue that undermines successful transfers of wealth is the *breakdown of trust and communication* *within the family unit.* This breakdown, in turn, leads to a failure in preparing the heirs for their responsibilities. These two elements combined cause the majority of wealth transition failures. This lack of communication, trust, and heir preparation enables weaknesses within the family to go uncorrected. Without open communication there can be no honest consensus on the mission/management of the estate. These differences, *because they were not detected and addressed prior to the transition,* create unavoidable friction within the family, resentment for the prior generation's impositions, and sow the seeds for private communication and gossip within the current generation. The heirs, if not equipped to deal with this mistrust, begin to have separate goals and concepts for the family's wealth. The basis for the erosion of the family unity and the family's financial strength is thus established as the precursor to another failed transition. Wealth, with its power to amplify (for better or for worse), becomes a destructive and divisive force in the lives of the children. The loss of unity weakens the family structure, opportunities for securing the family's economic position slip by, and the estate becomes a statistic among the 70% that fail.

The cures to avoid wealth transition failure: Like all "cures," they begin with a desire to avoid failure, followed by an understanding of what it takes to remedy or avoid failure, and concludes in a move to action. No one likes to admit that they are headed for a crash, especially when they are at the end of a first-generation wealth-building process. Pride of achievement sets in. No one wants to acknowledge that they have moved "out of balance" between family unity and family financial strength. That's why 70% of the wealth transitions fail! As the research indicates, the following are the critical differences between estates that transition successfully and those that do not:

- **Acknowledge that the odds of failure are simply too large to be ignored and decide to take action.** It is profoundly important to understand the difference between simply knowing what to do versus taking effective action to do it (Chapter 4).

- **Assess your current readiness for the transition** by taking the 10-Question Wealth Transition Checklist in Chapter 5. Score yourself (your wealth transition plan) and estimate your odds of success with respect to historical data.

- **Accept the results of your assessment,** and if you find that your score indicates your predicament is similar to those estates that have a high probability of failure, seek a more detailed assessment to pinpoint the problem areas (50 confidential questions — for all family members), also in Chapter 5.

- Based on the diagnosis, **seek outside assistance from professionals** *who specialize in preparing heirs and developing family unity in the process.* The process of selecting a coach is detailed in Chapter 6. Despite the literally hundreds of well-coached family transitions that we have examined, we have *not encountered* one situation where the total cost of coaching a family into a successful wealth transition *exceeded one percent of the wealth at risk.*

- As you proceed with a Family Wealth Mission Statement in hand, embark on a course of **preparing your heirs for wealth and responsibility.** The 10-question checklist in Chapter 7 identifies the factors that separate the prepared from the unprepared, with a resultant impact on the success or failure of the estate transition.

- **Assign the heir personal responsibility** as part of his/her own development process, including the consistent use and modeling of the family's values. Chapter 8 outlines those tasks for which the heir must take personal responsibility, and where the heir can benefit mightily from a relationship with a competent mentor.

- **Relentlessly pursue the concepts of measurement and evaluation** with respect to the heir's performance in managing the family assets. This needs to include regular communication, education of the non-active family members in understanding the business, and careful preparation of the next generation of steward/heirs. Chapter 9 deals with these issues and stresses avoidance of the "hero" syndrome.

This book recaps what 3,250 transitioned families revealed to us. It is their story, not our own. The facts are undeniable. In short, it boils down to a decision by current family leadership as to whether or not the family should seek professional assistance in order to manage the risks of transition they feel cannot be self-managed.

In spite of our research, the process of successfully transitioning wealth remains one of converting knowledge (of the research) into action (for the family). It is the responsibility of the family's current patriarch/matriarch or other leadership to decide how to use the information in this book.

You have taken a major step simply by converting your concerns or questions into the action of reading this book. That conversion of concern into action places you in the top 1% of successful families. The decision before you is what steps do you now wish to take to ensure that your estate transition becomes one of the 30% that succeed, rather than one of the 70% that fail? We wish the very best outcome for you, your family, and your professional advisors, as we have been doing for the past 39 years.

Roy Williams   *Vic Preisser*

for

The Leadership Family Institute © 2003

(a tax-exempt Foundation for Post-Transition Research and Education)

Appendix 1
Research Background

For a number of years, *The Williams Group* had substantial success in the estate and financial planning arena, primarily based on its *values-based estate* and financial planning process.

Financially successful clients kept asking us to help them with their heirs: "How do we prepare our children?" As *The Williams Group* client base grew nationwide, we saw excellent estate and financial *plans* fall apart when the owners died. This was in spite of the fact that the best legal, tax, and financial advisors were used to develop these plans.

In trying to find out what was behind this consistent pattern of failure, we began our research. We sought out legal and tax advisors, psychologists, and business consultants. We found that everyone, including *The Williams Group*, was focused on preservation, governance, and tax-reduction techniques.

The Executive Committee International (TEC) is an organization formed to help business owners learn from one another. Among the basic tenets of the organization are confidentiality, openness of communication, sharing, and willingness to learn from peers or guest speakers. TEC Chapters consist of 10 to 15 CEOs or business owners, none of which would be directly competitive. These chapters meet monthly to exchange information and develop deeper relationships. TEC chapters are sprinkled across the U.S. and worldwide. TEC has thousands of chapters, mostly representing medium- to large-sized (closely held) companies. Our research began by asking TEC groups what was successful or not successful in the transition of their own companies (or wealth). Some were second and third generation owners and others were founders or first generation. Over the next 20 years, *The Williams Group* interviewed 2,500 owners and clients (who may have managed only asset pools) to ascertain what worked and what did not.

As a member of TEC, Roy Williams was allowed to ask questions of members who would normally be unavailable to answer, or reluctant to answer from a non-peer. Because of the organizational and direct relationship, as well as the well-known confidentiality component of membership, Roy Williams found members very open in their responses.

In addition, the background of *The Williams Group* in estate and financial planning equipped Roy Williams to ask focused questions, and, depending on the response, to delve deeper into the answers to identify the core or causal issues. This included plans that evolved over time; for example, a buy-and-sell agreement, written 15 years prior, conflicted with a subsequent buy-and-sell agreement for another corporation (but for the same owners). Wills were written at a different junctures. Births, marriages, divorces, deaths, pledges of business assets - all events which regularly occurred - created unintentional conflicts.

These inconsistencies, or unaddressed issues, often appeared in the second or third generations, revealing what had not been anticipated at the time of the original planning.

A pattern emerged as a distinct set of consistent principles underlying both successful and failed estate transitions:

The first factor was a breakdown of communication within the family. This breakdown had its root cause in a lack of trust within the family. This was a consistent feature of almost all failed transitions. Examples of this would include the heirs being uninformed of the parental estate plan or transition plan, how much money the parents earned, or even the family's net worth. Yet family advisors had full access to such information, and the heirs knew of that access – which left the heirs with the feeling of being less trustworthy than the advisors. The parent(s) offered excuses such as, "I don't want to create a disincentive for them by letting them know how much they will inherit," or "If I tell them, all they will be waiting for is for me to die, so they can get the money." There were hundreds of excuses, but the underlying theme was *no trust*. Where trust did not exist, families consistently demonstrated very little open communication.

When *The Williams Group* began interviewing the second and third generations, they found the same problems were clearly recognized by heirs who stated, "Why didn't my Dad trust me enough to tell me what he had planned before he died, so I could be prepared?" or "My brother or sister have no interest or involvement in the business, and yet they own two-thirds of the company, receive two-thirds of the distributions, and resent my salary and company car - which are part of my employment with the family company!" Repeatedly, there was no clear understanding among the siblings (of failed transitions) concerning the concepts of "sweat equity" or the fact that a salary and perks would have to be paid to a non-family member employed in the business. While the stories were varied, the theme was the same: no trust, and therefore, little communication.

The second factor that emerged during these interviews was the lack of preparation of the heirs. Hardly any plans for the heirs were established, other than their attendance at a college. Many of the heirs learned of their role when the lawyer read the will, *after* Dad died. Almost all were totally unprepared. Many spent years trying to learn and made dreadful mistakes in hiring the wrong people to advise them. Some hired family professional advisors, only to learn that a good trial lawyer or good CPA auditor do not necessarily make good investment advisors, nor even know how to select one. The advisors may or may not have possessed any particular business skill in running a company.

Friends, family, and hangers-on earnestly tried to help. Their lack of competence in managing wealth resulted in the loss of the business and/or wealth. This created more mistrust and more miscommunication, lawsuits, and more problems and suspicious heirs mistrusting everyone.

In successful estate transitions, trust based on competence was reinforced by more trust and confidence in the heir's judgment. The need for control, stemming from a fear of loss of money, power, influence, etc., was offset over time by increasing trust. This manifestation of trust by the family leaders, in the judgment and competence of heirs, proved to be a stimulus to further efforts by the heirs to develop even better judgment and even more competence. It was a positive and affirming cycle that built on itself. This led to more open communication and disclosure of information. Accountability, reliability, and commitment were the ways the heirs were measured. Knowing this, standards were set and agreed on.

The third factor we found to be consistent (among failed transitions) was the lack of clarity in "roles" that might be available to the heirs in the management of family assets. This was especially harmful where heirs wished to make a contribution to the family, and demonstrated interest, yet no effort was made to match a role with their talents and interests. Mission and Strategy/Structure definitions would lead to the identification of possible roles for heirs. Without a strategy and structure set up to accomplish the (missing) mission for the family wealth, roles could not be clearly stated. With the absence of roles, no observable or measurable standards could be established for heirs to fulfill those roles. We found no business or family remained unified (in subsequent generations) where they did not share a common mission, common goals, common values, and an authentic trust. The steady rise in divorce rates and family dissolution are broader examples of this phenomenon.

Research Group Sizes, Participants

The family size researched ranged from one child to 22 children and spouses. The average of all 2,500 families was 3 children, with 1.5 being married – ages ranged from 8 to age 68.

Study 1 involved 2,500 individuals interviewed; 80% were leaders of closely held operating businesses and 20% were owners and managers of cash, securities, and real property interests. The families studied had net worth ranging from just under $5 million to well over $1 billion, with the average range between $15 million to $70 million. Of the families, 70% were first-generation and 30% were both second- or third-generation managers of wealth and/or business. The first-generation managers had a 20% divorce rate. The second- and third-generation managers had a 40% divorce rate. The largest family surveyed had 12 members and the smallest had 3 members (plus spouses and/or grandchildren). The geographic locations of the businesses surveyed were fairly distributed across the U.S. The primary locations were California, Texas, New York, and Florida.

Study 2 was a survey of 750 questionnaires sent to family-owned businesses throughout the Midwest.

This research, by Michael Morris, Ph.D., Miami of Ohio, Roy Williams, Ramon Avila, Ph.D. at Ball State and Jeff Allan, Ph.D. at the University of Central Florida, was published in the Journal of Business Venturing #8, 1997 Elsevier Science Press, titled: "Correlates of Success in Family Business Transitions." This survey confirmed the conclusions reached from the 2,500 individuals surveyed in Study #1, above. There were also eight large families from Canada included in the data before compiling the final results for the survey.

Appendix 2
Confidential
"Mountain" Family
Report

"MOUNTAIN" FAMILY POST-COACHING SCORING AND DIAGNOSIS: This report is preliminary and was completed only after the final of the six reports came in. Our understanding of this group is that it consists of six members of the same family, Mother and Father, as well as two children and their spouses. The questionnaires give no indication as to which member of the family completed them, and, accordingly, we submit a blind score.

SUMMARY: Looking at the summary data sheet, the following conclusions are indicated:

1. This family has made remarkable progress and is clearly in the top 30% of families and is likely to successfully transition their wealth.

2. To further secure that successful transition, the family can very productively spend time working on the following areas:

   a. Expanding their internal communications effectiveness to ensure that a more uniform understanding of who does what (now and especially in the future) is attained, and that the criteria for future planning decisions/changes are understood by all

b. Specific actions to further prepare the heirs by offering clear options to participate in the management of the family assets. This will help learning, may benefit from the use of mentor processes, and will give heirs the values/performance experience they must have.

TRUST AND COMMUNICATIONS: This family now scores fairly well, overall, with an average of 3.4 out of a perfect 5. Among the three major categories, at 3.4 Trust and Communications received the lowest overall score. One significant outcome worth working on, COMMUNICATIONS, merits further concentration. This variance between family members is as large as 57% and represents a real difference. It seems to be based, primarily, on the perceptions of communication. Family members varied from 0% feeling "uninformed" to as high as 20% "I don't know" answers. It is the area likely to be most productive to the family future relationships. The results in this category would suggest a formal process for communicating family estate and financial planning, as well as asset management and philanthropic information, within the family. Future family efforts might benefit from an emphasis on this particular area (written, periodic scheduled family meetings with specific agenda items, listening skills, etc.)

HEIR PREPARATION: The family scored a high average of 3.9 out of a perfect 5 in this category, indicating that most issues of heir preparation are being addressed. On the other hand, there was a variation of 21% in the individual family answers on this subject, which predicts a significant benefit if the topic of *developing heir competencies* is further addressed. Whether this is through focused use of mentors, or through the making of a *range* of possibilities available for family members to learn by managing family assets, both need to be revisited by this family.

MISSION AND STRUCTURE: This family scored 4.5 out of a perfect 5 in this area. It is an indication that all members understand the family mission, understand that roles are being defined and redefined as needed. There remains some uncertainly about *who is doing (or going to be doing) what.* Each heir's specific future roles and responsibilities are worth reemphasis in the future. The minimal variance of 15% says that, for the most part, this area is converging squarely on target.

Appendix 3
Sample Family Wealth Mission Statements

- To use our resources to strengthen our family and to support causes in which we believe.

- We are committed to family bonding, community outreach, and fun. We grow the family assets and provide for the family's education, growth, and security.

- To create an environment for making choices that benefit ourselves and the world for generations to come.

- To maximize the equitable transfer of my assets in a way that will enable and encourage my heirs to work for the benefit of humanity.

- Through God's grace, dream, plan, and grow closer to God and each other using the resources entrusted to our care for the benefit of God's work, family, business people, and community.

- To strengthen our family and use its assets wisely; to enable our family and others to realize their fullest potential; to value and encourage love, work, self-sufficiency, and cooperation within the family and in the larger community.

Appendix 4
Further Information

COACHING: Family Coaching and Heir Preparation (family wealth mission statements, improving communication skills, strengthening family loyalty, developing strategies, roles for heirs, mentoring, etc.) are available from *The Williams Group* on an individual family basis, conducted at their location of choice. To discover whether we may be of help, please call Roy or Vic directly, or contact them through the website below.

50 QUESTION TRANSITION READINESS SURVEY
@ 2001
A 50-question anonymous Survey, completed by *all family members and spouses*, submitted to *The Williams Group* for analysis and scoring. The result is a detailed written report of the differences within the family that threaten a successful post-transition. Anonymity of respondents is protected. All participating family members receive a copy of the 7 page customized report.
Cost: $500 per entire family of 7 (+$50/person beyond 7)

BOOK: "PHILANTHROPY HEIRS & VALUES" @ 2005
How Successful Families Are Using Philanthropy To Prepare Their Heirs for Post-Transition Responsibilities - After interviewing 3,250 families and examining almost 100 foundations, this book discloses how successful families use philanthropy as a teaching tool to improve their odds of post-transition success. Their children learn *Values*, develop appreciation for a specific *Mission* and are instilled with a sense of *Accountability*. The authors provide exercises, examples and checklists for each of 5 major age groups.
By: Roy Williams & Vic Preisser
Cost: $29.95 per copy + $4.50 shipping and handling

BOOK: "PREPARING HEIRS"@ 2003
Five Steps to a Successful Transition of Family Wealth and Values. Provides the reader with facts on the worldwide 70% failure rate of wealth transfers, accompanied by a series of checklists enabling comparison with 3,250 intensively studied families. Identifies rules for preparing heirs.
By: Roy Williams & Vic Preisser
Cost: $29.95 per copy + $4.50 shipping & handling

BOOK: "FOR LOVE & MONEY" @ 1995 *A Comprehensive Guide to the Successful Generational Transfer of Wealth.* Aids the reader by explaining the fundamentals of why wealth does not remain in family hands, supported with anecdotal stories of actual family situations.
By: Roy Williams
Cost: $29.95 per copy + $4.50 shipping & handling

Additional copies of this book and others by *The Williams Group* may be ordered through the Publisher, Robert D. Reed Publishers, or through *The Williams Group's* web site: *thewilliamsgroup.org*

The Williams Group
3620 W. Hammer Lane, Stockton, CA 95219
(209) 477-0600   website: *thewilliamsgroup.org*